Start With
Science

By BARBARA DONDIEGO
Illustrated by MARION HOPPING EKBERG and GARY MOHRMAN

Extend basic science activities with cross-curricular project books

Totline® Publications
A Division of Frank Schaffer Publications, Inc.
Torrance, California

Managing Editor: Kathleen Cubley
Editor: Marie Ianetti
Contributing Editors: Carol Gnojewski, Susan Hodges,
   Elizabeth McKinnon, Susan Sexton, Jean Warren
Copyeditor: Kris Fulsaas
Proofreader: Miriam Bulmer
Editorial Assistant: Durby Peterson
Graphic Designer (Interior): Sarah Ness
Graphic Designer (Cover): Brenda Mann Harrison
Illustrator (Cover): Kelly McMahon
Production Manager: Melody Olney

ISBN: 1-57029-171-1

Library of Congress Catalog Card Number 98-60798
Printed in the United States of America
Published by Totline® Publications
Editorial Office: P.O. Box 2250
                  Everett, WA 98203
Business Office: 23740 Hawthorne Blvd.
                  Torrance, CA 90505

20 19 18 17 16 15 14 13 12 11 10 9 8 7 6 5 4 3 2 1

Introduction

Start With Science provides your children with learning experiences to enjoy and remember. Inside, you will find instructions for 24 hands-on science projects, each accompanied by a 5-page reproducible take-home book. By completing a science project and then making a book about the experience, your children expore the natural world, record their observations, and review important skills. And the resulting project books become treasured keepsakes to share with friends and family!

Start with Science introduces children to the scientific method through investigations of topics such as plants, animals, and weather. Most of the projects are simple enough to complete in a single day. Each project includes a materials list and complete instructions. As your children work, stand by to offer individual help as needed. When the science projects are complete, your children will be ready to construct their take-home books.

Each take-home book contains reproducible activity pages that review and build upon the science projects. These unique skill sheets are to be completed over a series of days, providing practice in writing, counting, measuring, sequencing, and more. Step-by-step instructions appear on the left-hand side of each reproducible page. Take note of any steps that may require special assistance. Photocopy the book pages and gather necessary materials, such as writing or drawing supplies and glue. When the books are bound, these instructions will no longer be visible, and can be trimmed off if desired.

At home, parents will enjoy reading aloud the boldface text at the bottom of each page and talking with their child about the whole experience. *Start With Science* and build basic skills, enhance literacy development, and send home a delightful souvenir!

Contents

Activity Pages

Healthy Foods

You Will Need

- food guide pyramid
- pen
- chart paper
- old magazines
- scissors
- glue
- paper plates

Find a food guide pyramid and show it to your children. (You can find the pyramid on cereal boxes and other food packages.) With the children, discuss each category of the pyramid, then ask them to think of some healthy foods. Write their responses on chart paper and then reread them to the class.

As a follow-up activity, provide your children with old magazines, scissors, glue, and paper plates. Using the food pyramid as a guide, encourage them to cut out pictures from the magazines that represent a healthful meal. Then have each child glue his or her food cutouts to a paper plate.

Making My Healthy Me Book

1. Photocopy a set of pages 33–37 for each of your children.
2. Provide each child with a set of book pages. Read through the pages with your children, making sure they understand the activity directions on each page.
3. Have your children complete the activities, while you provide help as needed.
4. Invite the children to decorate their book covers. They may wish to draw healthy foods or glue magazine pictures of healthy foods on the cover.
5. Help your children arrange their book pages in order. Staple each book along the left-hand edge.
6. Have your children "read" their books to you and to one another. Encourage them to take home their books and share them with their families.

Feet As a Measuring Tool

You Will Need

- pencil
- heavy paper
- scissors
- masking tape
- classroom items
- paper

Invite your children to use their feet as a fun measuring tool. First have the children each remove one shoe and sock. Help them trace their bare foot on a sheet of heavy paper and then cut along the lines to make a foot cutout. Show them how to use a foot cutout to measure things around them such as the width of a door or table. Then have the children use their foot cutouts to measure items and record the measurements on a piece of paper.

Next, divide your children into pairs. Have one child in each pair stand against a wall while the other child uses masking tape to mark his or her height on the wall. Have them use their foot cutouts to measure their heights.

Talk with your children about where they think the measurement called a "foot" came from. Have them compare their foot cutouts. What would some of the problems be if a "foot" was each person's foot length rather than a standardized 12 inches?

Making My Footprints Book

1. Photocopy a set of pages 38–42 for each of your children.
2. Provide each child with a set of book pages. Read through the pages with your children, making sure they understand the activity directions on each page.
3. Have your children complete the activities, while you provide help as needed.
4. Invite the children to decorate their book covers. They may wish to draw feet on the cover.
5. Help your children arrange their book pages in order. Staple each book along the left-hand edge.
6. Have your children "read" their books to you and to one another. Encourage them to take home their books and share them with their families.

Discovering Textures

You Will Need

- crayons
- bags
- textured items

With your children, discuss different textures. Explain that texture is how something looks and feels. For example, things can be soft, smooth, rough, or bumpy to touch. Ask your children to think of other words that describe different textures. After your discussion, provide your children with their project book cover and crayons. Take them on a texture hunt. Have them find an object outdoors that has an interesting texture (tree bark, concrete, etc.). Have them place the book cover on top of the object and rub a crayon across it.

Extension: Divide your children into small groups. Provide each group with a shopping bag containing two samples each of the following items: cotton ball, corduroy, satin, sandpaper, burlap, silk, foil, and velvet. Let the children in each group take turns placing their hand in the bag, feeling a texture, and taking it out of the bag. Have them reach into the bag again to find the matching texture. Take turns until all of the textures have been experienced.

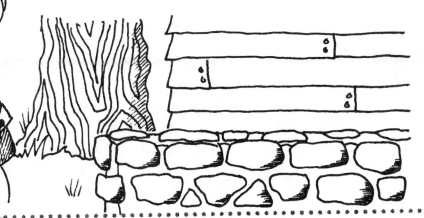

Making My Texture Book

1. Photocopy a set of pages 43–47 for each of your children.
2. Provide each child with a set of book pages and one piece of each of the following items: cotton ball, sandpaper, velvet, and burlap. Read through the pages with your children, making sure they understand the activity directions on each page.
3. Have your children complete the activities, while you provide help as needed.
4. Help your children arrange their book pages in order with the texture rubbing covers (see above) on top. Staple each book along the left-hand edge.
5. Have your children "read" their books to you and to one another. Encourage them to take home their books and share them with their families.

Listening for Sounds

You Will Need

- tape player
- cassette tape
- plastic containers with lids
- small items
- paper (optional)
- stickers (optional)

In advance, make a tape recording of different household and classroom sounds. For example, you might record such sounds as a doorbell chiming, an alarm clock ringing, paper tearing, and water dripping from a faucet. Play each sound for your children and have them try to identify it.

For a follow-up activity, create a sound-matching listening center. Collect an even number of empty plastic containers. Fill each pair of containers halfway with the same small items, such as paper clips, jelly beans, pennies, sugar, or metal bolts. Replace the lid on each container and cover the outside of each can with paper if you wish. To make the game self-checking, place matching stickers on the bottom of each matching pair of containers. Place the containers in a play center and invite small groups of children to visit the center. Have the children take turns shaking the containers to find the pairs that sound the same. To check their guesses, have them turn the containers over to look for matching stickers.

Making My Sound Book

1. Photocopy a set of pages 48–52 for each of your children.
2. Provide each child with a set of book pages. Read through the pages with your children, making sure they understand the activity directions on each page.
3. Have your children complete the activities, while you provide help as needed.
4. Invite the children to decorate their book covers. For example, they might glue on magazine cutouts of objects that make sounds.
5. Help your children arrange their book pages in order. Staple each book along the left-hand edge.
6. Have your children "read" their books to you and to one another. Encourage them to take home their books and share them with their families.

Living Things

You Will Need

- butcher paper
- old magazines
- scissors
- glue

Talk with your children about living things. Ask them to name some things that are living. How can they tell the things they name are living? (Living things can grow and change, for example.) Then, take your children on a walk outside. During the walk, ask your children to carefully examine the things they see. Point to certain objects along the way and ask the children if the objects are living or not. Then return to the classroom and divide the children into small groups. Provide each group with butcher paper, crayons, old magazines, scissors, and glue. Let the children look through the magazines and cut or tear out pictures of living things, then have each child make a collage of the pictures.

Making My Living Things Book

1. Photocopy a set of pages 53–57 for each of your children.
2. Provide each child with a set of book pages. Read through the pages with your children, making sure they understand the activity directions on each page.
3. Have your children complete the activities, while you provide help as needed.
4. Invite the children to decorate their book covers. For example, they might cover one side with drawings of living things and the other side with nonliving things.
5. Help your children arrange their book pages in order. Staple each book along the left-hand edge.
6. Have your children "read" their books to you and to one another. Encourage them to take home their books and share them with their families.

Plants Come From Seeds

You Will Need

- craft sticks
- marigold seeds
- plastic cups
- potting soil
- fine-point markers
- water
- rulers

Provide each of your children with a craft stick, a few marigold seeds, and a clear-plastic cup filled with a few inches of potting soil. Using fine-point markers, have your children personalize their craft stick. Ask your children to place their seeds in the soil, sprinkle 1/4 inch of soil over the seeds, and then mist the soil with water. Then have the children place their craft sticks in the soil near the edge of the cup. Place each cup near a sunny window and let the children water the soil as needed to keep it moist. Encourage your children to watch the progress of their seeds each day. As the seeds start to sprout, have your children use rulers to measure their plant's growth. Every few days, discuss the seeds' development with your children. How are they alike? (All are green.) How are they different? (Some are small, some grow slower, etc.) Are plants living or nonliving? How can you tell?

Making My Plant Book

1. Photocopy a set of pages 58–62 for each of your children.
2. Provide each child with a set of book pages. Read through the pages with your children, making sure they understand the activity directions on each page.
3. Have your children complete the activities, while you provide help as needed.
4. Invite the children to decorate their book covers. For example, they might frame the cover with flower or plant stickers.
5. Help your children arrange their book pages in order. Staple each book along the left-hand edge.
6. Have your children "read" their books to you and to one another. Encourage them to take home their books and share them with their families.

Investigating Seeds

You Will Need

- dried beans and seeds
- resealable plastic bags
- plastic-foam trays

In advance, collect a variety of seeds such as dried beans (coffee beans, lima beans, garbanzo beans) popcorn kernels, flower seeds, mustard seeds, and grass seeds. Ask your children to collect seeds from the fruits and vegetables they eat. Possibilities include oranges, pumpkins, grapefruit, and melons. Provide each child with a small resealable plastic bag, and venture outdoors for a seed hunt. Invite the children to find seeds from trees, grasses, and weeds, and place the seeds in their bags.

Upon returning to the classroom, have your children sort the seeds from the hunt, along with the other seeds from your collection, on different plastic foam trays. Help them to identify and label the seeds on each tray. Talk about the differences in the seeds: some are very small, some are very hard, some can float in the air, etc. Ask questions such as these: Do seeds move by themselves? What are some ways they move? (Stick to clothes, fall, blow in the wind, etc.) Why do some seeds move? (To have more room to grow.)

Making My Seed Book

1. Photocopy a set of pages 63–67 for each of your children.
2. Provide each child with a set of book pages. Read through the pages with your children, making sure they understand the activity directions on each page.
3. Have your children complete the activities, while you provide help as needed.
4. Invite the children to decorate their book covers. For example, they might frame the cover by gluing different seeds around it.
5. Help your children arrange their book pages in order. Staple each book along the left-hand edge.
6. Have your children "read" their books to you and to one another. Encourage them to take home their books and share them with their families.

Exploring Leaves

You Will Need

- paper bags
- newspaper
- heavy books

Provide each of your children with a brown paper bag and head outdoors for a leaf hunt. Ask them to search for leaves of various sizes, colors, and types. Have your children place the leaves they collect in their bags. After returning to the classroom, divide the children into small groups. Have each group compile their leaves and sort them according to characteristics such as shape, color, texture, and size.

After the activity, have them press their leaves by laying them between sheets of newspaper and placing heavy books on top. Allow the leaves to dry for several days. After the leaves are dry, provide each child with several leaves to complete the activities in their project books.

Making My Leaf Book

1. Photocopy a set of pages 68–72 for each of your children.
2. Provide each child with a set of book pages. Read through the pages with your children, making sure they understand the activity directions on each page.
3. Have your children complete the activities, while you provide help as needed.
4. Invite the children to decorate their book covers. For example, they might glue real leaves on it.
5. Help your children arrange their book pages in order. Staple each book along the left-hand edge.
6. Have your children "read" their books to you and to one another. Encourage them to take home their books and share them with their families.

Investigating Trees

You Will Need

- measuring tapes
- construction paper
- crayons
- magnifying glasses
- paper bags
- informational book about trees

Divide your children into pairs and give each pair a "tree investigation kit." (Prepare the kits by placing a measuring tape, a sheet of light-colored construction paper, crayons, and a magnifying glass in a paper bag.) Take the children outdoors and let them choose a tree to investigate. Have them use the measuring tape to measure the tree trunk's circumference. After measuring the trunk, help the children read the measurement and record it on the paper bag. Then, ask your children to collect leaves from their tree and place them in the bag. Next, have them hold the sheet of construction paper on the tree bark and rub a crayon over the paper to make a bark rubbing. Finally, encourage the children to examine the tree using the magnifying glass.

Upon returning to the classroom, read your children an informational book about trees. Talk about what the book says about trees. For instance, some trees have smooth bark and others have rough bark. Some trees are very tall. The shape of a tree's leaves help us decide what kind of tree it is. Invite your children to try to identify the type of tree they investigated.

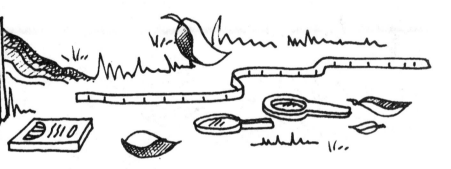

Making My Tree Book

1. Photocopy a set of pages 73–77 for each of your children.
2. Provide each child with a set of book pages. Read through the pages with your children, making sure they understand the activity directions on each page.
3. Have your children complete the activities, while you provide help as needed.
4. Invite the children to decorate their book covers. For example, they might frame the cover with tree stickers or stamps.
5. Help your children arrange their book pages in order. Staple each book along the left-hand edge.
6. Have your children "read" their books to you and to one another. Encourage them to take home their books and share them with their families.

Investigating Fruit

You Will Need

- fruit
- plastic knives
- paper plates

Take your children on a field trip to a local grocery store or farmer's market to shop for fresh fruit. Encourage the children to notice the different shapes, sizes, colors, and textures of the fruits. Purchase five or six different kinds of fruit, such as oranges, apples, grapefruit, bananas, pears, and strawberries.

Upon returning to the classroom, have the children compare and sort the fruit by type. Then provide the children with plastic knives and paper plates. Have them use the knives to slice the fruit. Assist the children in finding the seeds in each fruit. Set aside several of the seeds from the oranges, grapefruits, apples, and pears for planting. Point out that the bananas have very small brown seeds that we eat with the fruit, and that strawberries have tiny seeds on the outside of the fruit. Have your children taste a piece of each fruit. Talk about the sense of taste, and how foods may taste sweet, salty, sour, or bitter. Can the children name some foods that have these different tastes? How do we experience taste? (With our tongues.)

Making My Fruit Book

1. Photocopy a set of pages 78–82 for each of your children.
2. Provide each child with a set of book pages. Read through the pages with your children, making sure they understand the activity directions on each page.
3. Have your children complete the activities, while you provide help as needed.
4. Invite the children to decorate their book covers. For example, they might attach fruit stickers or magazine cutouts of fruit.
5. Help your children arrange their book pages in order. Staple each book along the left-hand edge.
6. Have your children "read" their books to you and to one another. Encourage them to take home their books and share them with their families.

Learning About Vegetables

You Will Need

- informational book about vegetables
- vegetables
- table knives
- bowls
- plastic forks
- salad dressing

With your children, look at pictures of growing plants that we eat. Talk about the different parts of plants—root, stem, leaf, and flower—and how they vary in appearance. Then, take your children to a local grocery store or farmer's market to examine and compare some harvested vegetables. Encourage your children to notice the different sizes, shapes, textures, and colors of the vegetables. Explain what root vegetables are (vegetables that grow underground, such as potatoes, carrots, and radishes) and have them examine a few. Then have them look at spinach, kale, and lettuce—vegetables that are leaves. Explain that an onion is a bulb that grows underground and that celery is actually a stem. Finally, have the children examine broccoli, cauliflower, and artichokes. Explain that we eat the flowers of these vegetables.

Extension: Bring in a variety of vegetables such as carrots, lettuce, celery, cucumbers, peppers, and an onion. Have the children wash and drain the vegetables. Provide them with table knives; have them cut the vegetables in small pieces and separate the lettuce into leaves. Encourage the children to use their senses to discover how the vegetables look, feel, sound when cut, and smell. Then have the children place all of the cut vegetables in a large bowl and toss them to make a salad. Divide the contents into individual bowls for each child. Provide each child with a plastic fork and some salad dressing and enjoy tasting the vegetables, too.

My Vegetable Book

Making My Vegetable Book

1. Photocopy a set of pages 83–87 for each of your children.
2. Provide each child with a set of book pages. Read through the pages with your children, making sure they understand the activity directions on each page.
3. Have your children complete the activities, while you provide help as needed.
4. Invite the children to decorate their book covers. For example, they might cover it with drawings or magazine cutouts of vegetables.
5. Help your children arrange their book pages in order. Staple each book along the left-hand edge.
6. Have your children "read" their books to you and to one another. Encourage them to take home their books and share them with their families.

Learning About Dogs

You Will Need

- dogs
- posterboard
- markers

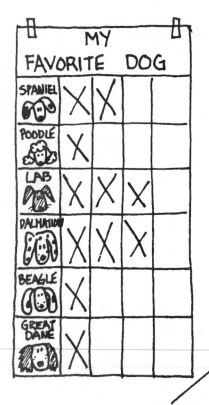

Provide an opportunity for your children to observe a variety of dogs. Invite local pet stores or animal shelters to bring in different types of dogs or puppies and tell your class about each breed. Or take a field trip to a veterinarian's office or an animal shelter. Have your children ask questions about the dogs, such as: What do they eat? How often do they eat? Do they have to have their hair cut? Invite your children to examine the similarities and differences among the dogs. Also provide pictures, posters, and reference books about dogs for your children to look through.

As a follow-up activity, make a class survey or graph on posterboard that includes six common varieties of dogs. Have your children vote for their favorite type of dog. Then examine the results of the graph and ask your children to determine which type of dog was their favorite. Make another graph that includes the following dog colors: gray, brown, white, black, and yellow. Have your children vote for their favorite color of dog. Have the children record the results on a piece of paper. Talk about how graphs are one way to show quantities without using numbers.

Making My Dog Book

1. Photocopy a set of pages 88–92 for each of your children.
2. Provide each child with a set of book pages. Read through the pages with your children, making sure they understand the activity directions on each page.
3. Have your children complete the activities, while you provide help as needed.
4. Invite the children to decorate their book covers. For example, they might attach magazine cutouts of different breeds of dogs, or draw their favorite dog.
5. Help your children arrange their book pages in order. Staple each book along the left-hand edge.
6. Have your children "read" their books to you and to one another. Encourage them to take home their books and share them with their families.

Keeping an Eye on Spiders

You Will Need

- nonfiction books about spiders
- spider web
- clear jar with lid

What better way to teach your children about spiders than to give them hands-on experience with the eight-legged little critters? Start by reading several nonfiction books about spiders to your children. Talk about how most spiders are safe to observe, but a few kinds should be avoided because their bite is poisonous. What kind of poisonous spiders live in your area? Also talk about how spiders help our environment by eating insects. Where do spiders live? Are their webs their houses?

Then, with a clear glass or plastic jar with a lid, take children outdoors in the morning to find dew-covered spider webs. Have them examine the webs and notice that little spiders build little webs and big spiders build big webs. Inform them that some spiders build webs that look like blankets and others build webs that resemble the spokes of a wheel. Have the children look for insects on the web. Talk about what the spiders do with these insects they catch (they eat them). Then, try to transfer a few spiders into the jar for the children to get a closer look at them. Have the children count the legs on the spiders and help them notice the creatures' physical characteristics. When the children are through observing the spiders, help them return them to their natural environment.

Making My Spider Book

1. Photocopy a set of pages 93–97 for each of your children.
2. Provide each child with a set of book pages. Read through the pages with your children, making sure they understand the activity directions on each page.
3. Have your children complete the activities, while you provide help as needed.
4. Invite the children to decorate their book covers. For example, they might frame the cover with spider drawings.
5. Help your children arrange their book pages in order. Staple each book along the left-hand edge.
6. Have your children "read" their books to you and to one another. Encourage them to take home their books and share them with their families.

Learning About Butterflies

You Will Need

- butterfly kit
- reference books
- pictures
- posters

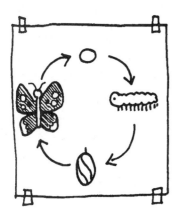

To give your children firsthand experience studying butterflies, purchase a butterfly kit, available at some children's specialty stores or science stores (or call Insect Lore at 800-LIVE-BUG). Talk with your children about how a butterfly starts its life as a caterpillar. The caterpillar turns into a soft pupa, and a hard covering called a chrysalis forms over it. Inside the chrysalis, the pupa develops into a butterfly. When it is fully formed, the butterfly emerges from the chrysalis, dries its wings, and flies away. Inform your children that having the butterfly nursery in the classroom allows them to see the life cycle of the caterpillar, but normally this cycle would happen outdoors on a leaf. Provide reference books, pictures, and posters about butterflies, and encourage your children to look through the materials. Read aloud books about the life cycle and stages of a butterfly. When your butterfly emerges from its chrysalis, encourage the children to examine its three body parts (head, thorax, and abdomen). Have them also notice the four wings, six legs, and balled antennae.

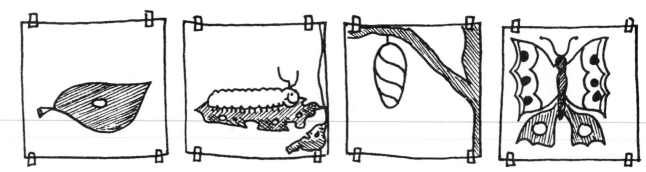

Making My Butterfly Book

1. Photocopy a set of pages 98–102 for each of your children.
2. Provide each child with a set of book pages. Read through the pages with your children, making sure they understand the activity directions on each page.
3. Have your children complete the activities, while you provide help as needed.
4. Invite the children to decorate their book covers. For example, they might frame the cover with butterfly stickers or stamps.
5. Help your children arrange their book pages in order. Staple each book along the left-hand edge.
6. Have your children "read" their books to you and to one another. Encourage them to take home their books and share them with their families.

Learning About Ladybugs

You Will Need

- ladybugs (or a ladybug kit)
- glass container
- plastic wrap
- tape

Visit the local public or school library and check out books and magazines with information about ladybugs. Share the following interesting facts about ladybugs with your children: ladybugs are also knows as "ladybird beetles"; they are considered friends of gardeners because they eat aphids and other insects that might be harmful to plants; each ladybug has a different number of spots on its back; and not all ladybugs are "ladies"—some are male and some are female.

Introduce your children to these friendly creatures by purchasing some live ladybugs at a garden store. Place them in a glass container and have your children help you place a sheet of plastic wrap over the top of the container and secure it with tape. To provide fresh air to the ladybugs, poke a few small holes in the plastic wrap. (You can also order ladybug kits from Insect Lore. Call 800-LIVE-BUG for information.) When your children are through observing the ladybugs, release them into a garden.

Making My Ladybug Book

1. Photocopy a set of pages 103–107 for each of your children.
2. Provide each child with a set of book pages. Read through the pages with your children, making sure they understand the activity directions on each page.
3. Have your children complete the activities, while you provide help as needed.
4. Invite the children to decorate their book covers. For example, cover them with drawings of ladybugs.
5. Help your children arrange their book pages in order. Staple each book along the left-hand edge.
6. Have your children "read" their books to you and to one another. Encourage them to take home their books and share them with their families.

Discovering Shadows

You Will Need

- yarn
- chalk
- scissors
- paper bags

In advance, place a length of yarn, a piece of chalk, and scissors in a paper bag for each of your children. Then introduce the children to shadows by taking them outdoors on a sunny day. Encourage them to examine their own shadows as well as those of their friends. Invite them to find shadows of other items, such as trees, bushes, buildings, and fences. Then discuss the shadows your group sees. Talk about the position of the sun, the size of the shadows, and so on. Have your children locate the biggest and smallest shadow they can see.

Next, divide your children into pairs and have them stand on pavement. Have the children in each pair use chalk to trace around each other's shadow. Then have them measure their drawings, using the length of yarn, and cut off the excess yarn. Ask your children to compare their measuring strings to see which children have the same size yarn, the largest piece, and the smallest piece. Let your children repeat the measuring activity several hours later to compare the results. Are the shadows the same size?

Making My Shadow Book

1. Photocopy a set of pages 108–112 for each of your children.
2. Provide each child with a set of book pages. Read through the pages with your children, making sure they understand the activity directions on each page.
3. Have your children complete the activities, while you provide help as needed.
4. Invite the children to decorate their book covers. For example, they might cover them with a drawing of themselves and their shadows.
5. Help your children arrange their book pages in order. Staple each book along the left-hand edge.
6. Have your children "read" their books to you and to one another. Encourage them to take home their books and share them with their families.

Investigating Water

You Will Need

- pen
- chart paper
- cups
- balance scale
- water
- towels

Ask your children about all the ways that they use water and where they think it comes from. Write their responses on chart paper. Then help them discover that water has weight. Place a plastic cup on each end of a balance scale. Have a child fill one of the cups with water. What happens to the scale? Explain that because the water is heavy and has weight, it causes the scale to move. Then divide the children into pairs and give one child in each pair two bath towels. Have the children in each pair take turns holding out their arms to resemble a balance scale, holding one towel in each hand. Have them soak one of the towels in water, and then wring out the towel. Let the children hold the wet towel in one hand and the dry towel in the other hand. The children will discover that the wet towel is heavier because water has weight.

Making My Water Book

1. Photocopy a set of pages 113–117 for each of your children.
2. Provide each child with a set of book pages. Read through the pages with your children, making sure they understand the activity directions on each page.
3. Have your children complete the activities, while you provide help as needed.
4. Invite the children to decorate their book covers. For example, they might create a border of drawings of water droplets.
5. Help your children arrange their book pages in order. Staple each book along the left-hand edge.
6. Have your children "read" their books to you and to one another. Encourage them to take home their books and share them with their families.

Exploring Bubbles

You Will Need

- bucket
- liquid dishwashing detergent
- glycerin
- measuring cup
- measuring spoons
- water
- spoon
- plastic mesh berry baskets
- plastic six-pack holders
- paper towel tubes
- baking pans

Gather a clean bucket, liquid dishwashing detergent, glycerin (available at drug stores), a measuring cup and spoons, and water. Let your children help you make a batch of bubble solution. Combine 1 cup of liquid dishwashing detergent, 3 to 4 tablespoons of glycerin, and 8 cups of water. Gently stir the mixture with a spoon, cover it, and allow it to sit overnight.

The next day, provide your children with gadgets appropriate for bubble blowing such as berry baskets, plastic six-pack holders, and paper towel tubes. Pour the bubble solution into several baking pans and take your children outdoors. Have them dip their bubble blowers into the bubble solution and blow bubbles. Encourage them to discover many different ways to make bubbles.

My Bubble Book

Making My Bubble Book

1. Photocopy a set of pages 118–122 for each of your children.
2. Provide each child with a set of book pages. Read through the pages with your children, making sure they understand the activity directions on each page.
3. Have your children complete the activities, while you provide help as needed.
4. Invite the children to decorate their book covers. For example, they might cover it with drawings of bubbles.
5. Help your children arrange their book pages in order. Staple each book along the left-hand edge.
6. Have your children "read" their books to you and to one another. Encourage them to take home their books and share them with their families.

Magnet Fun

You Will Need

- magnetic wands
- magnetic items
- magnetic marbles
- nonmagnetic items
- magnetic surfaces

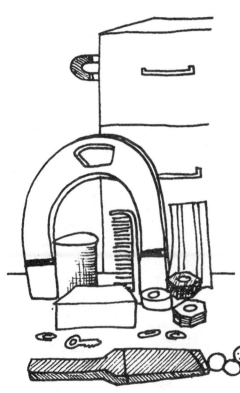

Divide your children into small groups. Provide each group with a magnetic wand (or other magnets) and a collection of items such as paper clips, magnetic marbles, keys, plastic combs, wooden blocks, and fabric swatches (if desired, include other objects that contain iron). Let the children use the magnetic wands to explore which objects in the collection are attracted to the magnet. Have them discover how many magnetic marbles their magnet can pick up at one time and compare their findings to other members of the group. Then invite the children to use the wands to explore items in the classroom such as a steel filing cabinet. What do objects attracted to the magnets have in common? (They are made of metal.) Have each group discuss their findings. Set out a nonmagnetic item, such as an aluminum can. Will the magnets stick to the can? (No, because magnets don't stick to aluminum.) Let your children discover that two magnets held together will attract or repel each other.

Extension: Give your children opportunities to discover that magnets will also attract objects through other objects, such as air. Supply each group with a paper clip. Have the children take turns laying a paper clip on a flat surface such as a desk or table. Then have them place the magnetic wand above the paper clip. Children will discover that the clip will move through the air toward the magnet.

Making My Magnet Book

1. Photocopy a set of pages 123–127 for each of your children.
2. Provide each child with a set of book pages. Read through the pages with your children, making sure they understand the activity directions on each page.
3. Have your children complete the activities, while you provide help as needed.
4. Invite the children to decorate their book covers. For example, they might draw magnets on them or make magnet prints with magnets dipped in paint.
5. Help your children arrange their book pages in order. Staple each book along the left-hand edge.
6. Have your children "read" their books to you and to one another. Encourage them to take home their books and share them with their families.

Discovering Rocks

You Will Need

- nonfiction books about rocks
- small rocks
- magnifying glasses
- egg cartons
- pen
- index cards

Invite your children to hunt for rocks around the school grounds. Then divide your children into small groups. Provide each group with magnifying glasses, books about rocks, and egg cartons. Have each group combine their rocks and use their magnifying glasses to carefully examine the rocks. Let each group sort their rocks in the egg cartons. Then have the children describe their rocks, using words such as "hard," "heavy," "rough," "smooth," "big," and "small." Write their words on index cards. Lay the cards on a table and have the children place their rocks near the cards that describe them.

Encourage your children to look through the nonfiction books and try to label some of the types of rocks in their cartons. Follow up with a discussion about some of the rocks' characteristics. What color are they? Are they rough or smooth? Are they rounded or angular? Are they heavy or light? What senses do we use to examine rocks? (Touch, sight.)

Making My Rock Book

1. Photocopy a set of pages 128–132 for each of your children.
2. Provide each child with a set of book pages. Read through the pages with your children, making sure they understand the activity directions on each page.
3. Have your children complete the activities, while you provide help as needed.
4. Invite the children to decorate their book covers. They may wish to draw rocks on the cover.
5. Help your children arrange their book pages in order. Staple each book along the left-hand edge.
6. Have your children "read" their books to you and to one another. Encourage them to take home their books and share them with their families.

Discovering Patterns in Nature

You Will Need

- paper bags
- nature items
- construction-paper strips
- glue

To introduce or review the concept of patterns, explain that a pattern is a design or picture that repeats. Show your children different examples of patterns in your classroom. For example, some children may be wearing patterned clothing. Then provide each of your children with a paper bag and head outdoors to collect things in nature such as flowers, pine cones, acorns, and leaves that have patterns. Have the children place their items in their bag. Upon returning to the classroom, have them empty the contents of their bag. Let them examine the patterns in each of the objects. Then provide the children with several construction-paper strips. Have them glue or lay the items on a strip to make a simple A-B-A-B pattern. Have them repeat the activity, making a different pattern each time.

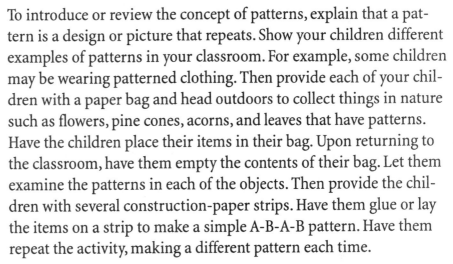

Making My Nature Book

1. Photocopy a set of pages 133–137 for each of your children.
2. Provide each child with a set of book pages. Read through the pages with your children, making sure they understand the activity directions on each page.
3. Have your children complete the activities, while you provide help as needed.
4. Invite the children to decorate their book covers. They may wish to draw flowers, trees, fruits, and so on.
5. Help your children arrange their book pages in order. Staple each book along the left-hand edge.
6. Have your children "read" their books to you and to one another. Encourage them to take home their books and share them with their families.

Learning About Weather

You Will Need

- chart or calendar
- white paper
- stapler
- pen
- crayons
- posterboard
- glue

In advance, make a weather chart of different pictures to symbolize different types of weather (sunny, windy, rainy, and snowy). Then, staple 11 blank white pages together for each child to make a booklet. Label the front of each booklet cover with "My Weather Journal." Then ask your class to name different types of weather. Each day, observe and discuss the weather with your class and mount the pictures on your chart or a calendar. Then have your children write about and draw the daily weather in their journal. Continue to observe and record the weather for ten days. Have the children predict the weather for the following day. After ten days, count the number of sunny, rainy, snowy, and windy days. Have your children determine which weather patterns were most and least frequent.

Extension: Have your children use crayons or markers to draw a picture to represent their favorite type of weather. Label a sheet of posterboard with headings such as "rainy," "sunny," "snowy," and "windy." Then have the children glue their picture under the corresponding heading, and discuss the graph results.

Making My Weather Book

1. Photocopy a set of pages 138–142 for each of your children.
2. Provide each child with a set of book pages. Read through the pages with your children, making sure they understand the activity directions on each page.
3. Have your children complete the activities, while you provide help as needed.
4. Invite the children to decorate their book covers. They may wish to glue on cutouts of pictures that represent different types of weather.
5. Help your children arrange their book pages in order. Staple each book along the left-hand edge.
6. Have your children "read" their books to you and to one another. Encourage them to take home their books and share them with their families.

Learning About Wind

You Will Need

- spray bottle
- construction paper
- markers
- crayons
- ruler
- stapler
- hole punch
- yarn
- glue
- streamers

Invite your children to go outside on a windy day and examine the different things that wind moves. While outdoors, ask the children to talk about what they see moving, such as leaves, tree branches, the hair on their heads, a flag, and flowers. On anther windy day, fill a spray bottle with water and go outside. Spray one hand of each child. Let the children discover that the wind dries and cools their hands. Talk about what senses they use to decide if the wind is blowing. (They can hear it; they can feel it; they can see it moving things.) Can they smell the wind? Taste it?

Extension: Have each of your children make a windsock. Provide each child with a large sheet of construction paper, markers, and crayons. Encourage them to use the markers and crayons to decorate their papers. Then have them fold down 1 inch on the long edge of the paper, which will be the top of the windsock. Demonstrate how to bend the paper into a cylinder shape, and staple it together. Use a hole punch to make three evenly spaced holes around the folded portion. Then tie a 15-inch piece of yarn to each hole and tie the ends of the yarn together at the top. To complete the project, have the children glue tissue-paper or crepe-paper streamers to the bottom of the windsock. Encourage the children to take their windsocks outside and fly them on a windy day.

Making My Wind Book

1. Photocopy a set of pages 143–147 for each of your children.
2. Provide each child with a set of book pages. Read through the pages with your children, making sure they understand the activity directions on each page.
3. Have your children complete the activities, while you provide help as needed.
4. Invite the children to decorate their book covers. For example, they might want to draw pictures of things being blown by the wind, such as clouds, a kite, or a flag.
5. Help your children arrange their book pages in order. Staple each book along the left-hand edge.
6. Have your children "read" their books to you and to one another. Encourage them to take home their books and share them with their families.

Exploring Rain

You Will Need

- tape
- rulers
- clear-plastic containers
- marker
- pen
- paper
- black construction paper

Have each of your children tape a ruler to the side of a clear-plastic container. Have the children label the bottom of the container with their name. Place the containers outside on a rainy day. At the end of the day, or after a few rainy days, have the children find their container and examine the amount of water in it. Have them record how much water is in their containers.

Extension: On a day when it is gently raining, provide each of your youngsters with a sheet of black construction paper. Then take them outdoors and have them hold their papers in the rain so that a few droplets fall on the paper. After a minute or so, return to the classroom. Have the children examine their papers to see if all of the raindrops look the same. Are they different shapes and sizes? How many drops are big and how many are small? Then have them count all of their raindrops and write down the total number of raindrops, and save it for their project books.

Making My Rain Book

1. Photocopy a set of pages 148–152 for each of your children.
2. Provide each child with a set of book pages. Read through the pages with your children, making sure they understand the activity directions on each page.
3. Have your children complete the activities, while you provide help as needed.
4. Invite the children to decorate their book covers. They may wish to draw raindrops on the cover.
5. Help your children arrange their book pages in order. Staple each book along the left-hand edge.
6. Have your children "read" their books to you and to one another. Encourage them to take home their books and share them with their families.

Discovering Rainbows

You Will Need

- prisms
- flashlights
- white paper
- bubble solution
- bubble wands

Introduce your children to the colorful concept of rainbows by having them make one themselves. Divide your children into small groups. Provide each group with a prism, a flashlight, and a sheet of white paper. Have one child in each group shine a flashlight beam through the prism, while another child holds the sheet of paper above the prism so that the color spectrum appears on the paper. Have each group carefully examine the results. Ask each group what colors they see and how the colors are the same as or different from those of a rainbow.

As a follow-up activity, take your children outside on a sunny day and have them dip a bubble wand into some bubble solution (see recipe on page 24) and begin to blow bubbles. Have them look at the bubbles and look for rainbows in the bubbles. Upon returning to the classroom, have the children complete the project book.

Making My Rainbow Book

1. Photocopy a set of pages 153–157 for each of your children.
2. Provide each child with a set of book pages. Read through the pages with your children, making sure they understand the activity directions on each page.
3. Have your children complete the activities, while you provide help as needed.
4. Invite the children to decorate their book covers. They may wish to draw a rainbow on the cover.
5. Help your children arrange their book pages in order. Staple each book along the left-hand edge.
6. Have your children "read" their books to you and to one another. Encourage them to take home their books and share them with their families.

Take-Home Books

My Healthy Me Book

By _____

1. Draw a
picture of
your favorite
healthy
foods.

These are my favorite healthy foods.

© 1998 Totline® Publications
(reproducible) p34

1. Color the
picture.
2. Fill in the
blank.

I brush my teeth _____ times a day.

2

	Mon.	Tues.	Wed.	Thurs.	Fri.	Sat.	Sun.
I exercise							
I eat healthy food							
I am well rested							
I am clean							

1. Put an X on the correct boxes.

I have healthy habits.

3

1. Glue a tissue
on the hand,
and recite
the poem.

A tissue I will use
Whenever I cough or sneeze.
Then I'll wash my hands
To keep them nice and clean.

(reproducible) p37

My Footprints Book

By _____

1. Trace around
your foot
cutout.

2. Color the
foot picture.

This is my footprint.

I can use it to measure.

1. Measure your classroom door and your chair with your footprint.

2. Fill in the blank.

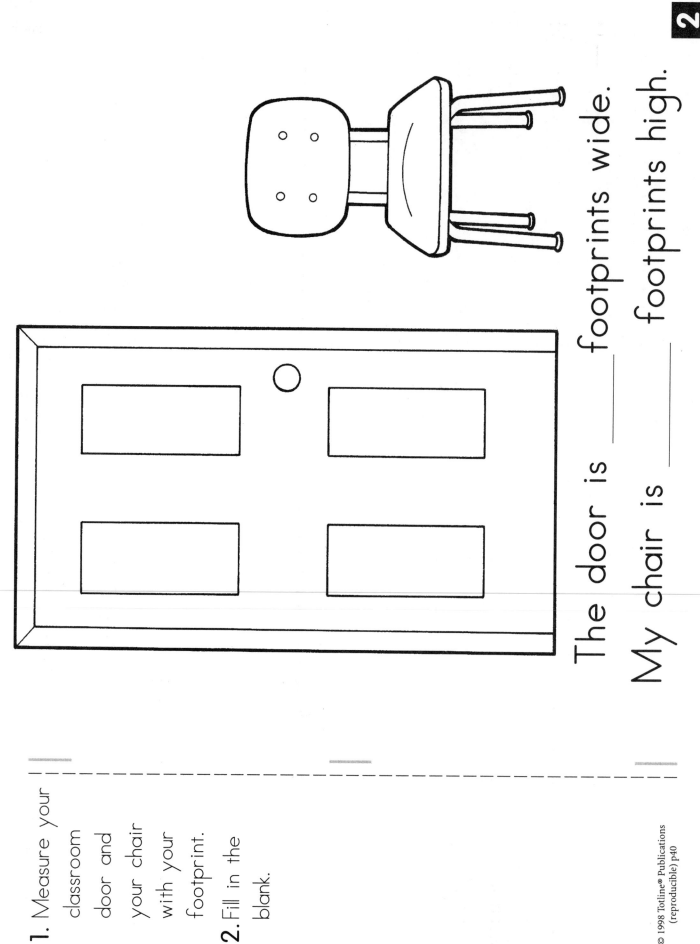

The door is _____ footprints wide.

My chair is _____ footprints high.

© 1998 Totline® Publications
(reproducible) p40

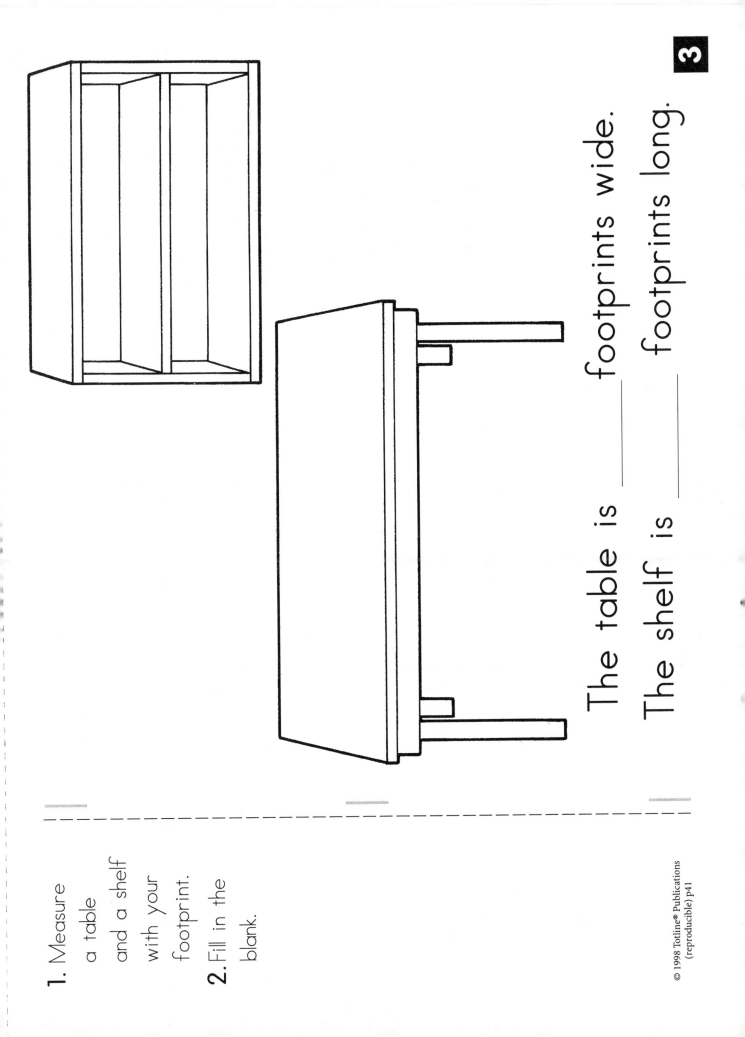

1. Measure a table and a shelf with your footprint.
2. Fill in the blank.

The table is _____ footprints wide.

The shelf is _____ footprints long.

3

© 1998 Totline® Publications (reproducible) p41

1. Read the rhyme.

One foot, two feet,
Now comes three;
I measure everything I see.

One foot, two feet,
Now comes three;
My little foot
Is so handy!

My Texture Book

By _____

1. Glue a
   cotton ball
   on this page.

2. How does
   the cotton
   ball feel?
   Write the
   word.

The cotton ball feels

_____

1.

1. Glue a piece of sandpaper on this page.

2. How does the sandpaper feel? Write the word.

The sandpaper feels _____.

1. Glue a piece
   of velvet on
   this page.
2. How does
   the velvet
   feel? Write
   the word.

The velvet feels

_____

3

1. Glue a piece
   of burlap on
   this page.

2. How does
   the burlap
   feel? Write
   the word.

The burlap feels _____

4

My Sound Book

By

1. Circle the
things you
can hear.

These things make sounds.

1. Draw
something
that makes a
quiet sound.

This makes a quiet sound.

1. Draw
something
that makes a
loud sound.

This makes a loud sound.

© 1998 Totline® Publications
(reproducible) p51

Sounds All Around

Sung to: "Frère Jacques"

There are sounds,
There are sounds
All around,
All around.
Loud sounds and quiet sounds,
High sounds and low sounds.
There are sounds
All around!

1. Sing the song.

My Living Things Book

By _____

These things are living.

1. Draw some
living things.

People are living things.

1. Draw a person.

1. Circle the living things.
2. Color the pictures.

These are living things.

1. Color the things that grow.

Living things grow and change.

© 1998 Totline® Publications
(reproducible) p57

My Plant Book

By _____

1. How many
   seeds did
   you plant?
   Write the
   number.

2. Color the
   picture.

I planted _____ seeds.

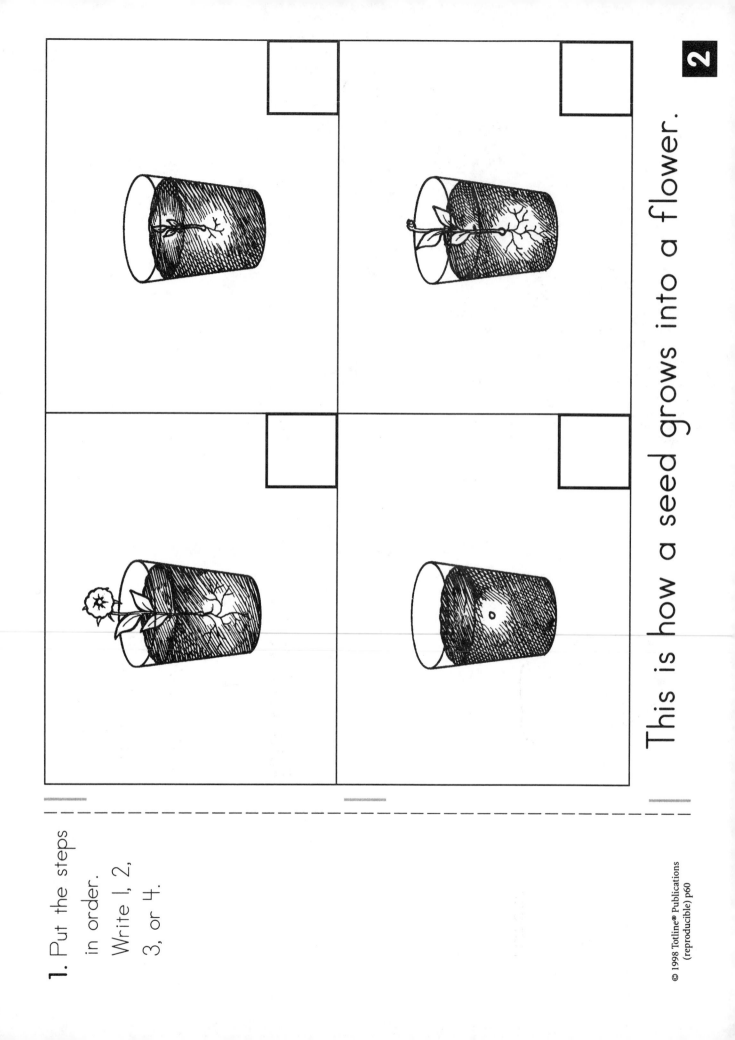

1. Put the steps in order. Write 1, 2, 3, or 4.

This is how a seed grows into a flower.

2

1. Read the rhyme.
2. Count the seeds.
3. Write the number.

Counting Seeds

I planted one seed,

Then two more,

Then another,

Now I have _____.

3

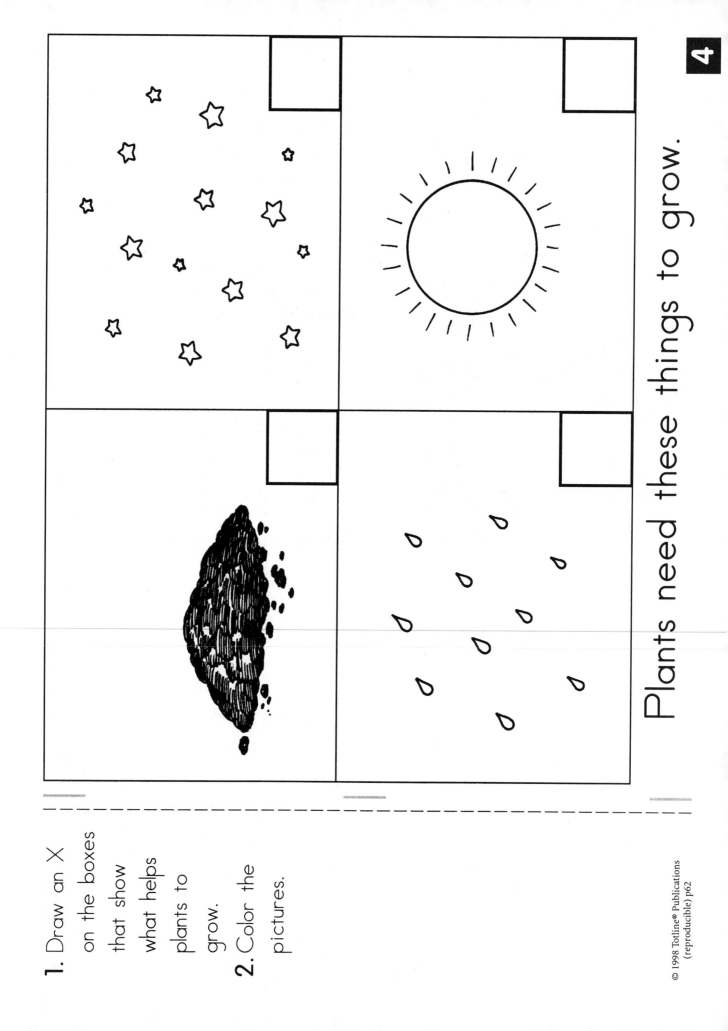

Plants need these things to grow.

1. Draw an X on the boxes that show what helps plants to grow.

2. Color the pictures.

4

My Seed Book

By _____

I have lots of seeds.

1. Draw your
seeds.

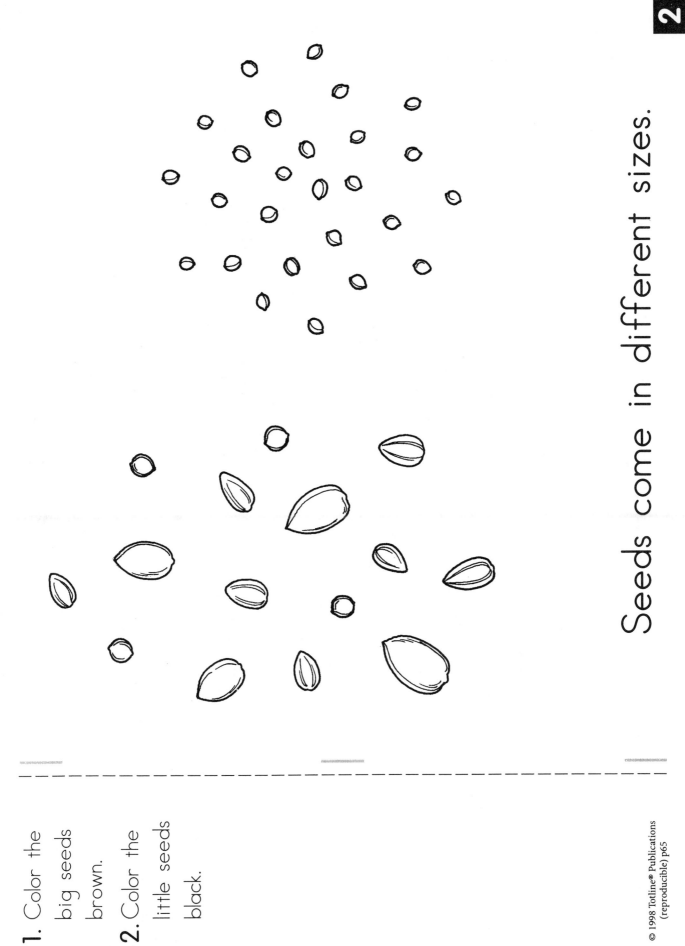

Seeds come in different sizes.

1. Color the big seeds brown.

2. Color the little seeds black.

© 1998 Totline® Publications
(reproducible) p65

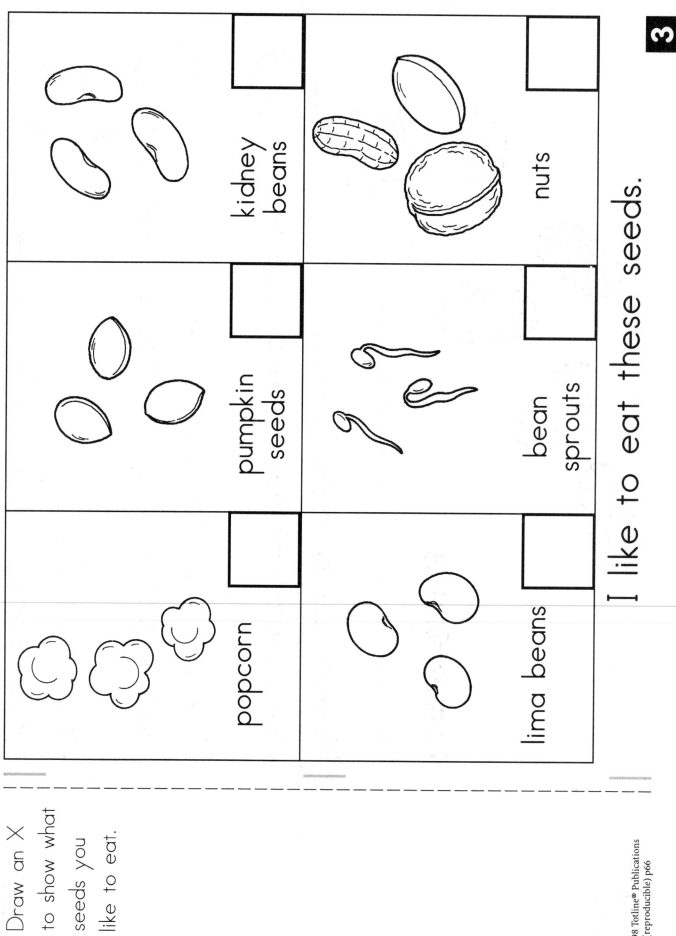

1. Draw an X to show what seeds you like to eat.

kidney beans	pumpkin seeds	popcorn
nuts	bean sprouts	lima beans

I like to eat these seeds.

1. Sing the
song.

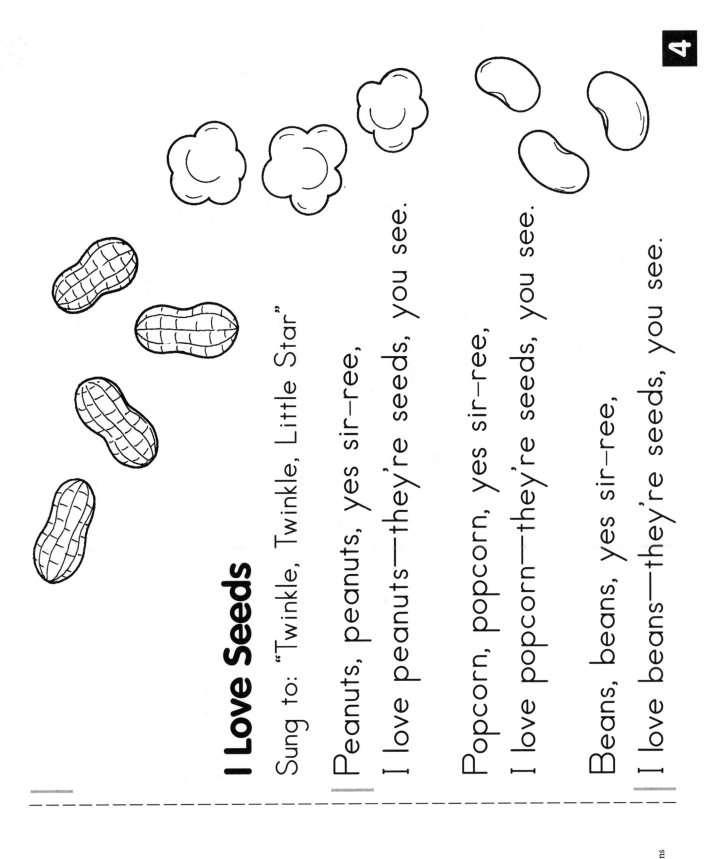

I Love Seeds

Sung to: "Twinkle, Twinkle, Little Star"

Peanuts, peanuts, yes sir—ree,

I love peanuts—they're seeds, you see.

Popcorn, popcorn, yes sir—ree,

I love popcorn—they're seeds, you see.

Beans, beans, yes sir—ree,

I love beans—they're seeds, you see.

© 1998 Totline® Publications
(reproducible) p67

My Leaf Book

By _____

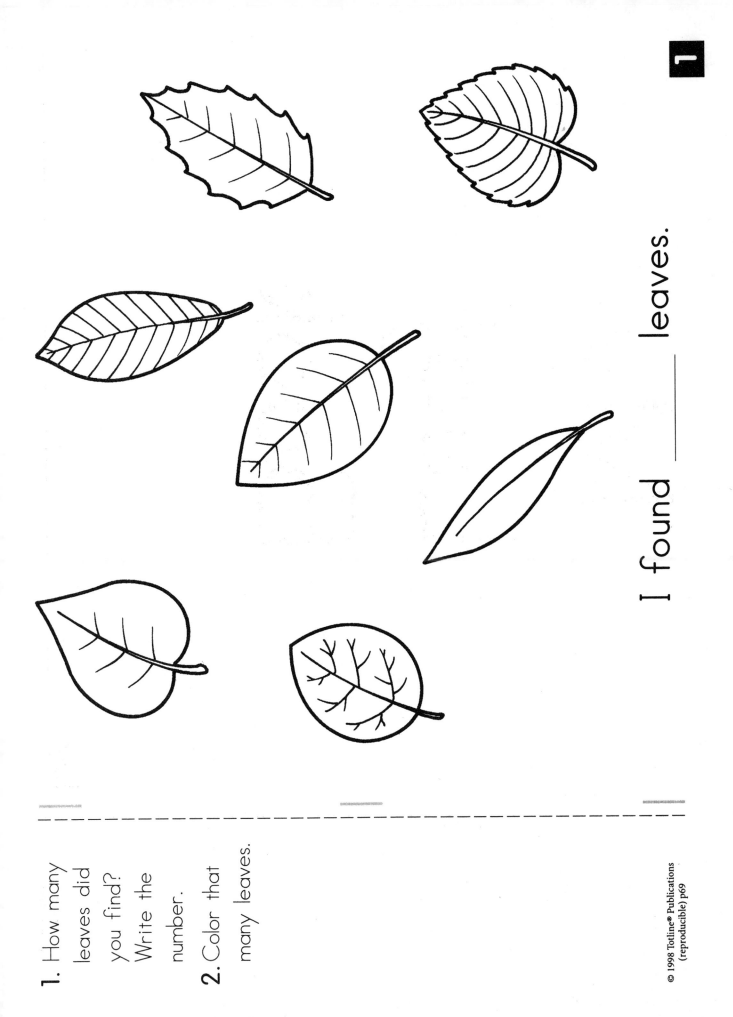

I found _____ leaves.

1. How many leaves did you find? Write the number.
2. Color that many leaves.

1. Use a ruler to measure your shortest leaf.

2. Fill in the blank.

My shortest leaf is _____ inches long.

© 1998 Totline® Publications
(reproducible) p70

2

1. Trace around
your favorite
leaf.

My favorite leaf is this shape.

Leaves, leaves falling down.
Red, yellow, orange, and brown.

1. Read the rhyme.
2. Color the leaves red, yellow, orange, and brown.

© 1998 Totline® Publications
(reproducible) p72

My Tree Book

By _____

1

My tree looks like this.

1. Draw your
tree.

© 1998 Totline® Publications
(reproducible) p74

1. How many inches around is your tree? Write the number.

2. Color the picture.

My tree is _____ inches around.

1. Glue a leaf
from your
tree on this
page.

This is a leaf from my tree.

1. Read the rhyme.

2. Draw a picture of you and your tree.

Tree Poem

I gave my tree a hug today,

And then what do you know?

A gentle breeze blew the leaves.

The branches waved hello.

My Fruit Book

By _____

1. What is your favorite fruit? Write the word.

2. Draw a picture of your favorite fruit.

My favorite fruit is _____.

1

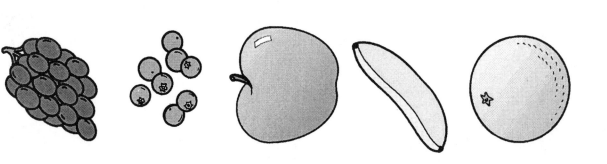

1. Color the crayons.
2. Draw lines to match the crayons with the fruits.

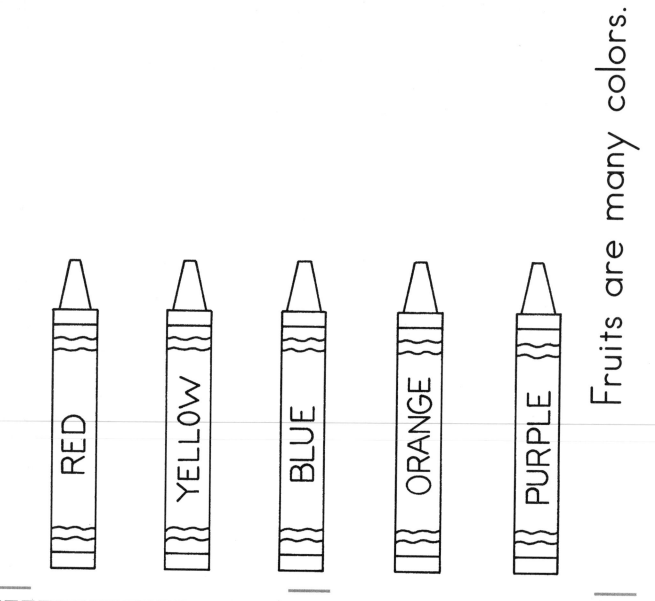

RED

YELLOW

BLUE

ORANGE

PURPLE

Fruits are many colors.

2

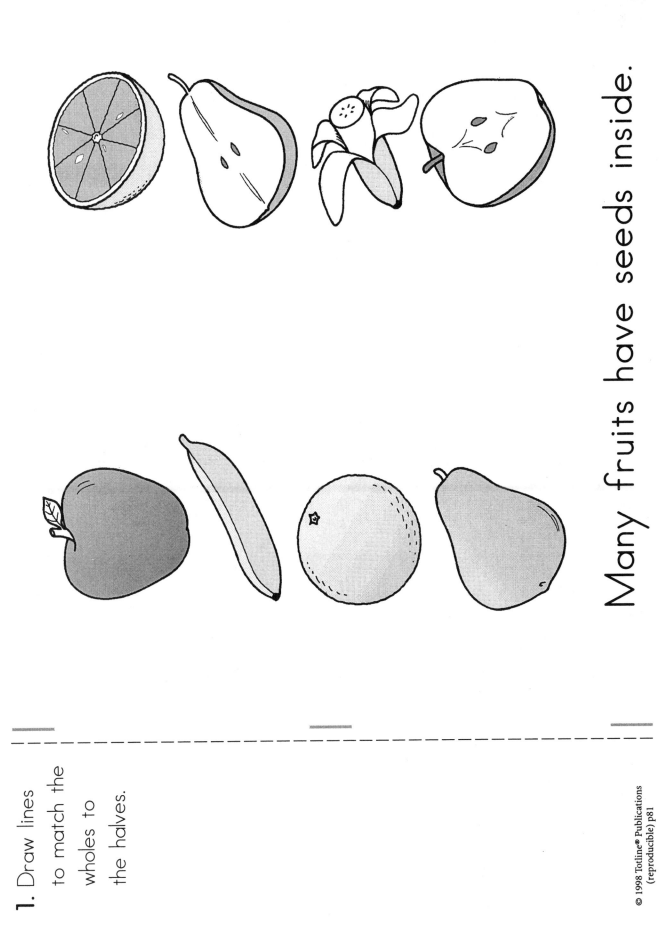

Many fruits have seeds inside.

1. Draw lines to match the wholes to the halves.

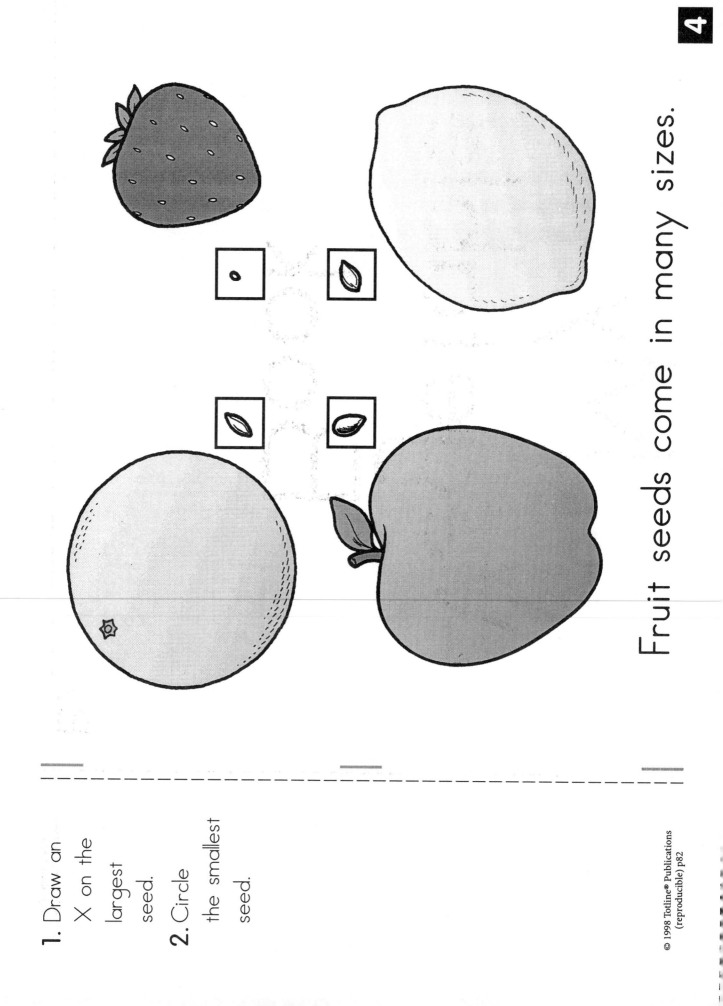

1. Draw an X on the largest seed.

2. Circle the smallest seed.

Fruit seeds come in many sizes.

4

My Vegetable Book

By _____

1. Circle the vegetables with flowers we eat.

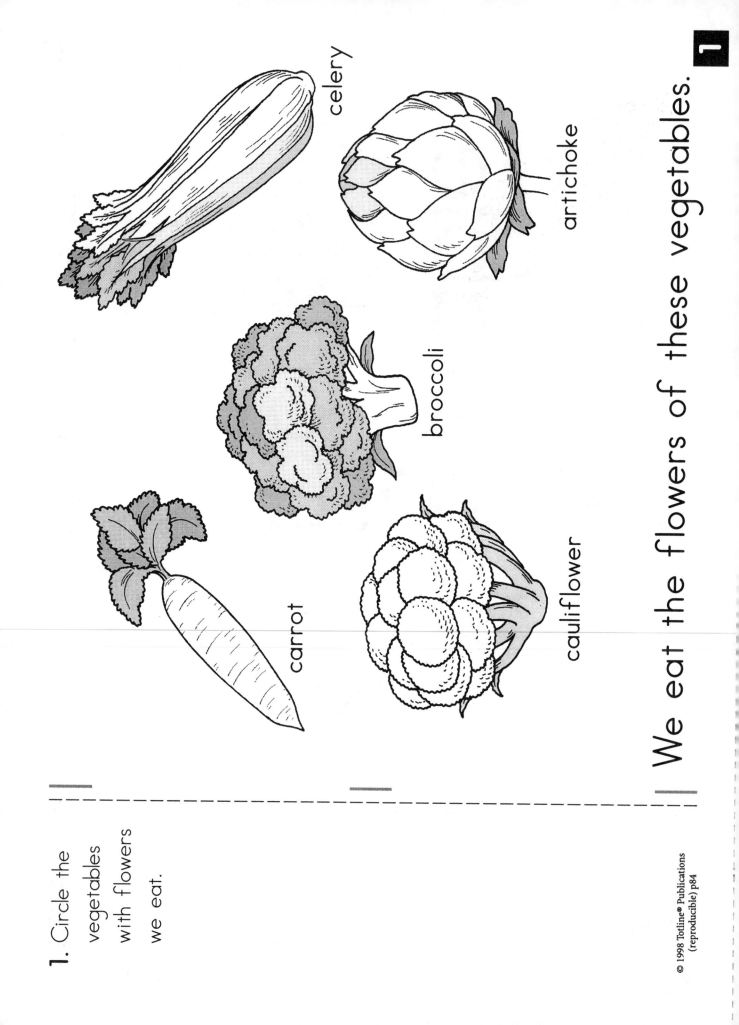

celery

artichoke

broccoli

carrot

cauliflower

We eat the flowers of these vegetables.

1

1. Circle the
vegetables
that are
roots.

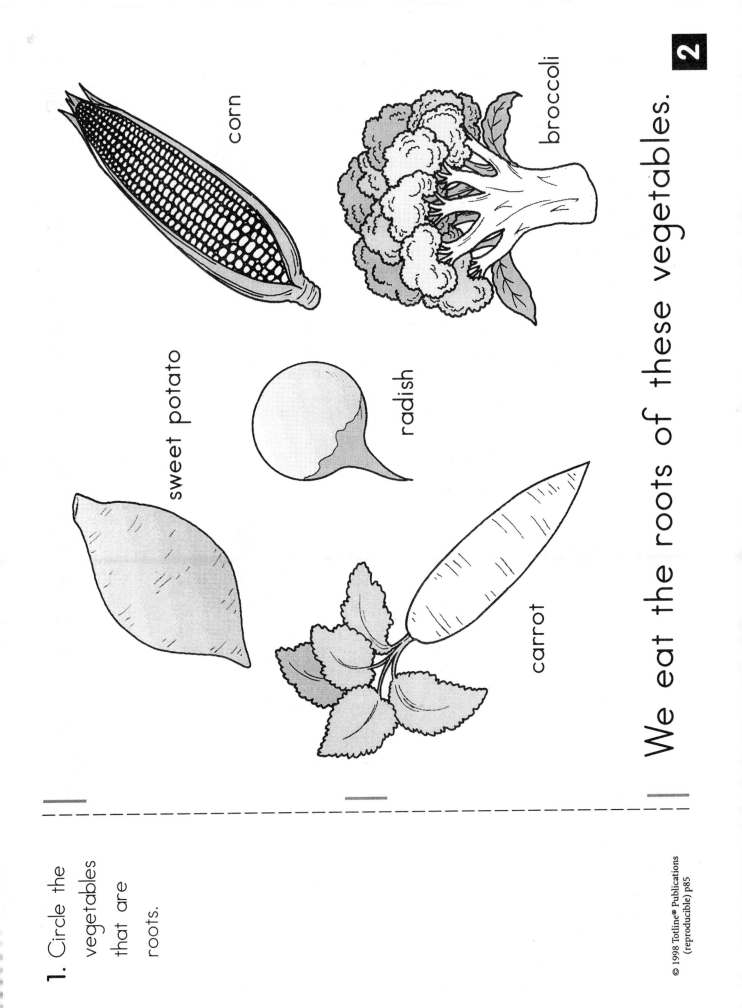

corn

broccoli

sweet potato

radish

carrot

We eat the roots of these vegetables.

© 1998 Totline® Publications
(reproducible) p85

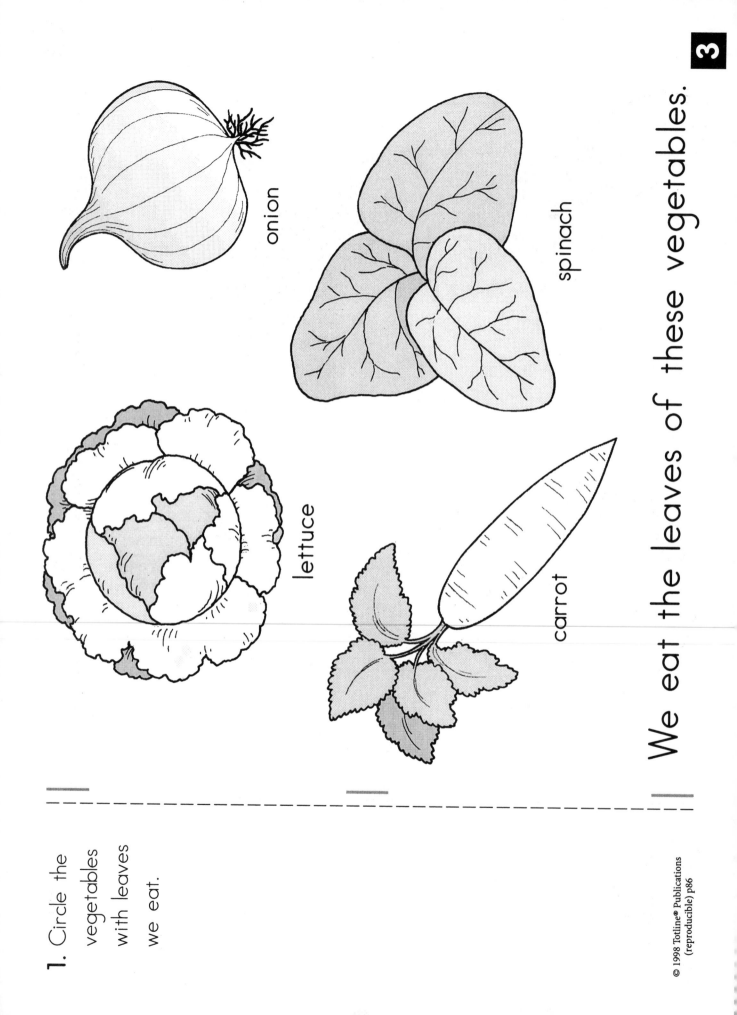

1. Circle the vegetables with leaves we eat.

onion

spinach

lettuce

carrot

We eat the leaves of these vegetables.

3

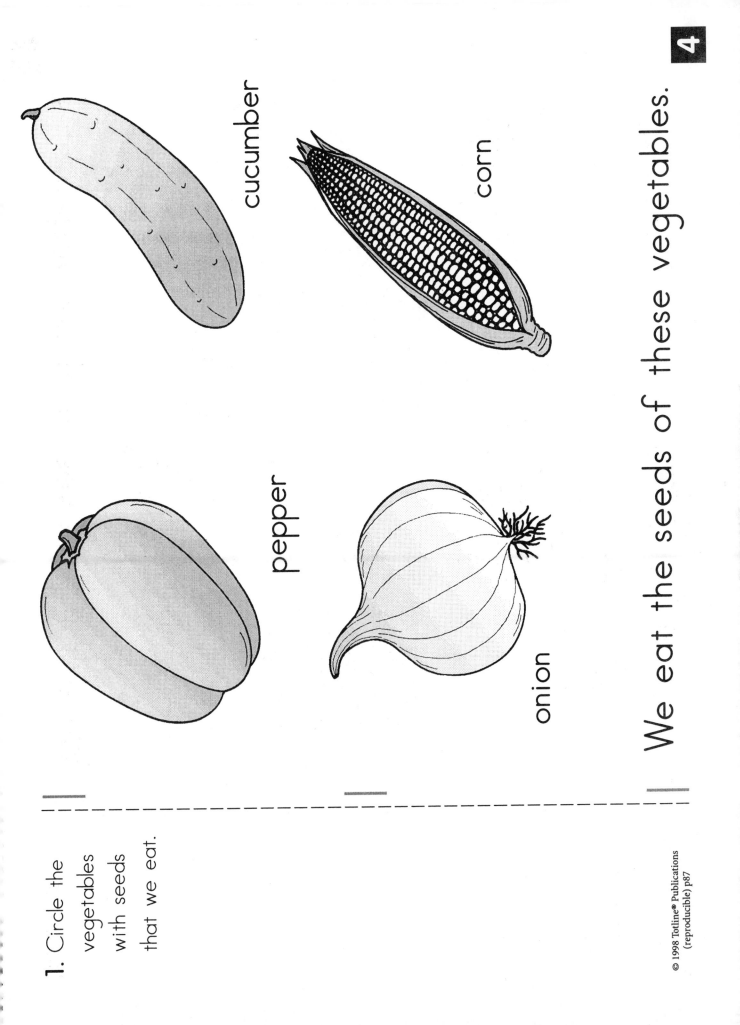

1. Circle the
vegetables
with seeds
that we eat.

cucumber

corn

pepper

onion

We eat the seeds of these vegetables.

4

My Dog Book

By _____

1. Circle your favorite dog.

2. Write the breed on the line.

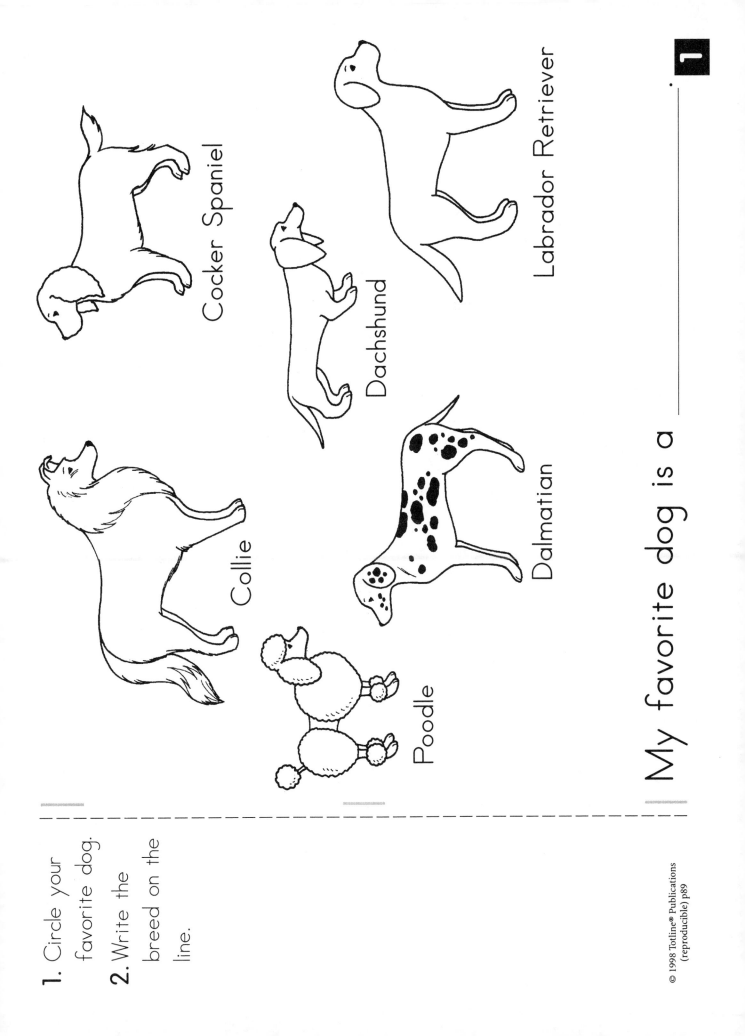

Cocker Spaniel

Dachshund

Labrador Retriever

Collie

Dalmatian

Poodle

My favorite dog is a _____

1. Match the
puppies
to their
mothers.

Bulldog

Poodle

Dalmatian

I helped the puppies find their mothers.

Favorite Dogs

Poodle			
Collie			
Cocker Spaniel			
Dalmatian			
Dachshund			
Labrador			

1. Ask five friends to vote for their favorite dog.

2. Write an X on the chart to record each vote.

3. Circle the dog with the most votes.

3

Dog Colors

gray									
brown									
white									
black									
yellow									

Our class likes _____ dogs best.

1. Copy the votes from your class dog survey on this page.

2. Which dog color is the favorite? Write the word.

© 1998 Totline® Publications
(reproducible) p92

My Spider Book

By _____

1. Draw a
spider web.

I found a spider web. It looked like this.

1

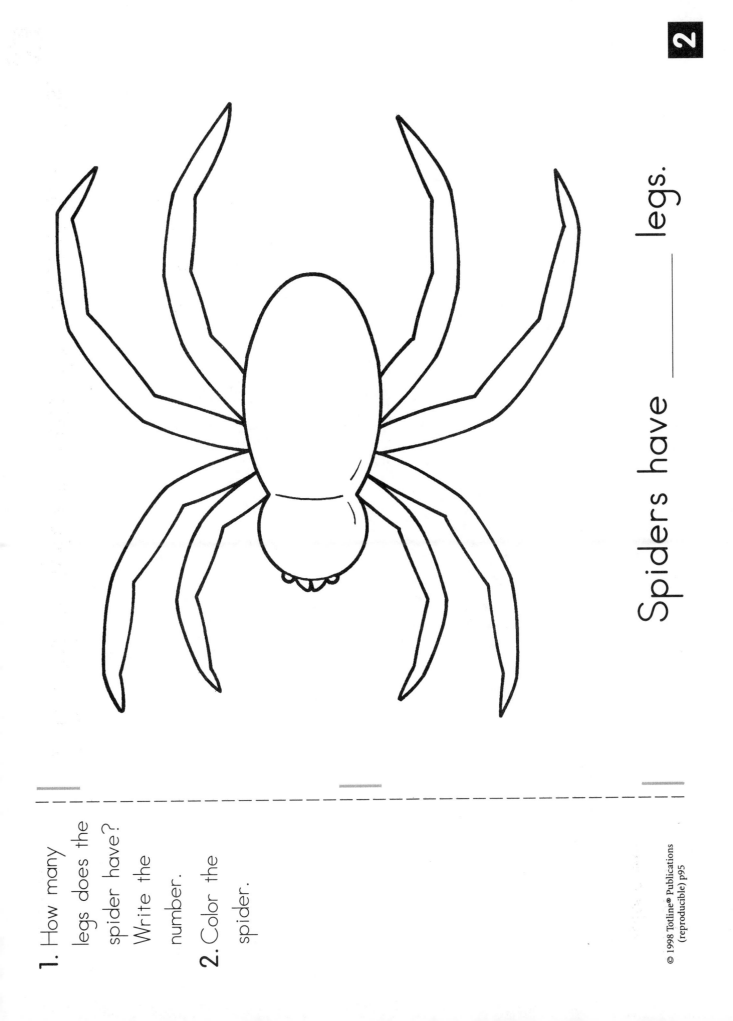

1. How many legs does the spider have? Write the number.

2. Color the spider.

Spiders have _____ legs.

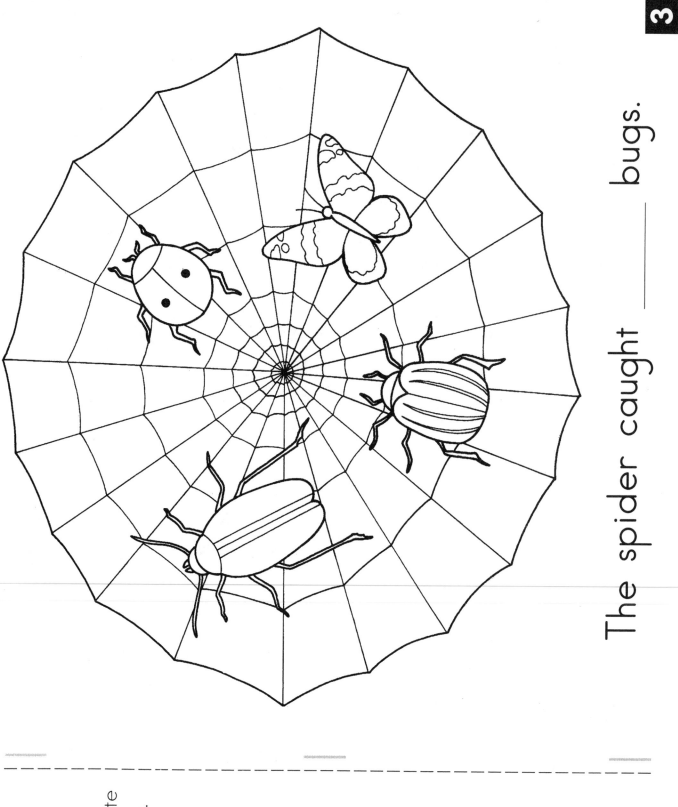

The spider caught _____ bugs.

1. How many
bugs did
the spider
catch? Write
the number.

© 1998 Totline® Publications
(reproducible) p96

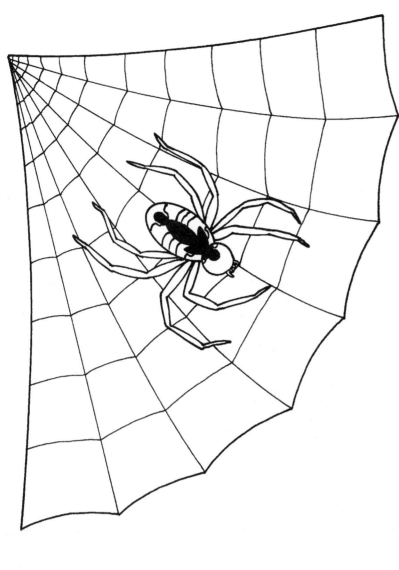

1. Read the rhyme.

Little Spider

I have eight legs
And lots of eyes.
I spin a sticky web
To catch bugs by surprise!

© 1998 Totline® Publications
(reproducible) p97

My Butterfly Book

By

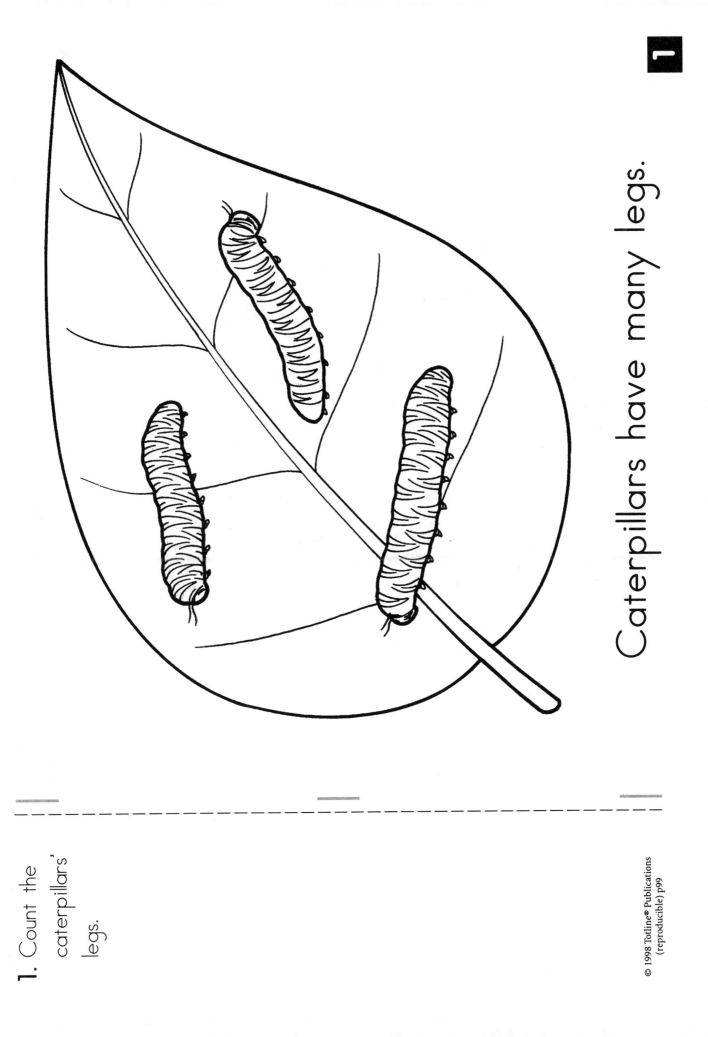

Caterpillars have many legs.

1. Count the caterpillars' legs.

1. Color the
picture.

The caterpillar turns into a chrysalis.

1. Color the
picture.

A butterfly hatches from the
chrysalis and flies away.

3

1. Read the rhyme.

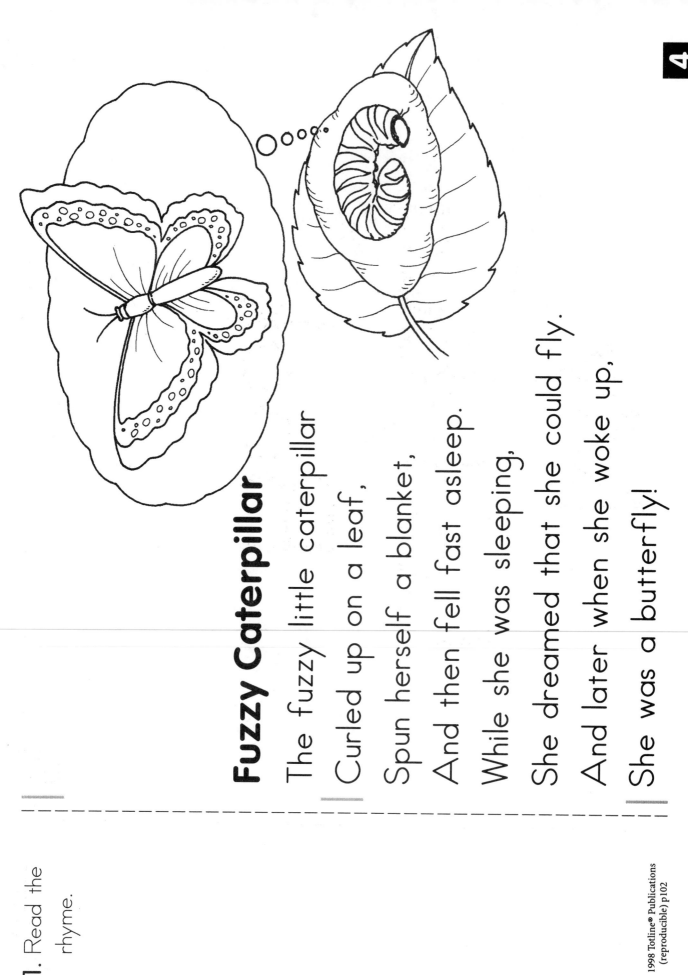

Fuzzy Caterpillar

The fuzzy little caterpillar

Curled up on a leaf,

Spun herself a blanket,

And then fell fast asleep.

While she was sleeping,

She dreamed that she could fly.

And later when she woke up,

She was a butterfly!

My Ladybug Book

By _____

Our ladybugs look like this.

1

1. Draw a
picture
of your
ladybugs.

1. Draw matching spots on the ladybugs' wings.

Ladybugs have matching wings.

© 1998 Totline® Publications (reproducible) p105

1. Draw
ladybugs
in the air.

Ladybugs can fly.

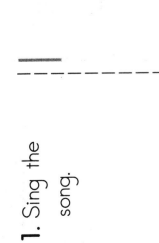

1. Sing the song.

My Ladybug

Sung to: "Twinkle, Twinkle, Little Star"

My ladybug, how I love you.

You're round and red and tiny too.

Little black spots on your shell,

You crawl and fly so very well.

Oh, oh, oh, look at you go!

Flying high and crawling low.

My Shadow Book

By _____

1. Put the steps
in order.
Write 1, 2,
3, or 4.

This is how I measured my shadow.

1. Measure your yarn.
2. Write the number.

My shadow was _____ inches long.

© 1998 Totline® Publications
(reproducible) p110

2

1. Draw lines to match the objects to their shadows.

I found the shadows.

3

1. Read the rhyme.

My Shadow

I go outside to see

How my shadow plays with me.

It jumps with me.

It runs with me.

It has lots of energy.

My Water Book

By _____

1. Color the
picture.

Water is everywhere.

1

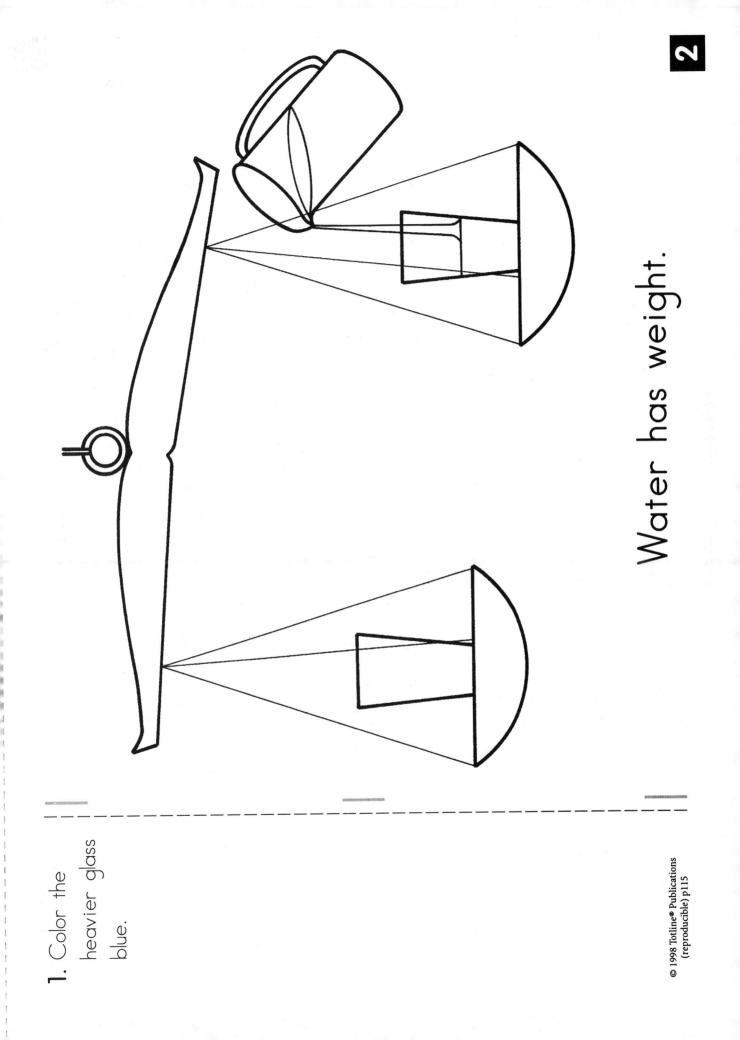

1. Color the
   heavier glass
   blue.

Water has weight.

1. How do you use water? Draw a picture.

I use water.

1. Read the
   rhyme.

Water

Water, water, everywhere,

To wash my face, to wash my hair.

Water comes from the sky,

Raindrops falling in my eye.

Water, water, in lakes and streams,

Making everything turn green.

My Bubble Book

By _____

1. Read the rhyme.
2. Count the bubbles.
3. Write the number.

I have a bubble on my finger,
And one on my nose.
I have one on my shoulder,
And one on my toe.
How many do I have in all?

The clown has _____ bubbles.

© 1998 Totline® Publications (reproducible) p119

1. How many
bubbles are
on each
wand? Write
the number.

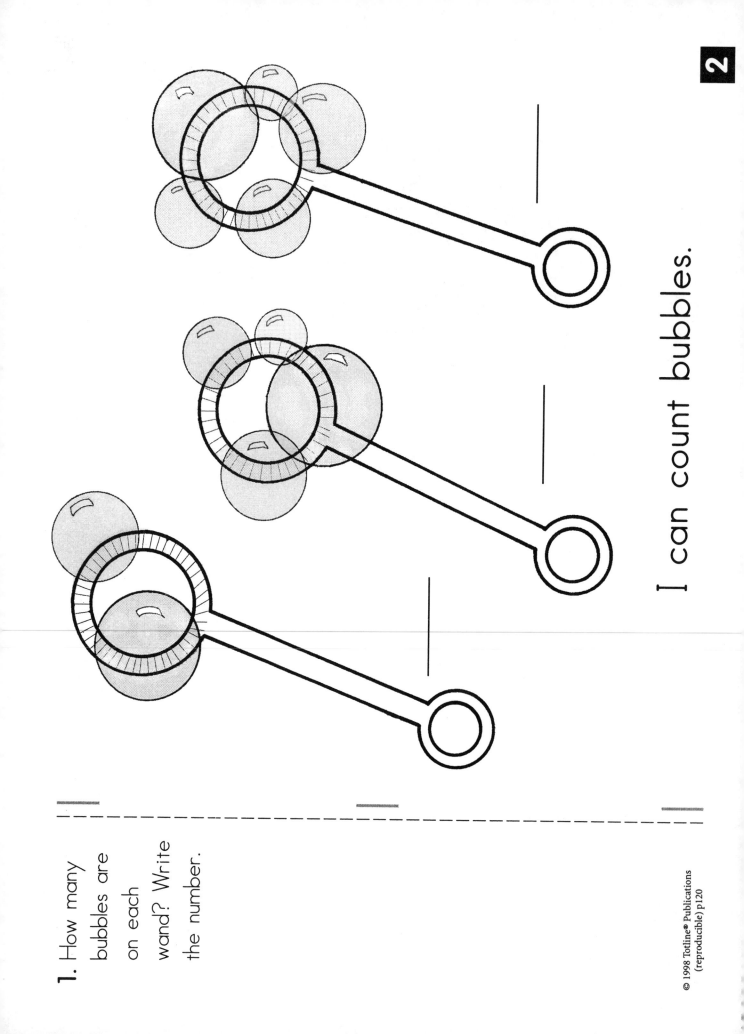

I can count bubbles.

1. Draw your
biggest
bubble on
the wand.

My biggest bubble was this big.

1. Draw your
smallest
bubble on
the wand.

My smallest bubble was this big.

4

My Magnet Book

By _____

1. Circle the pictures of things that a magnet sticks to.

A magnet sticks to these things.

1

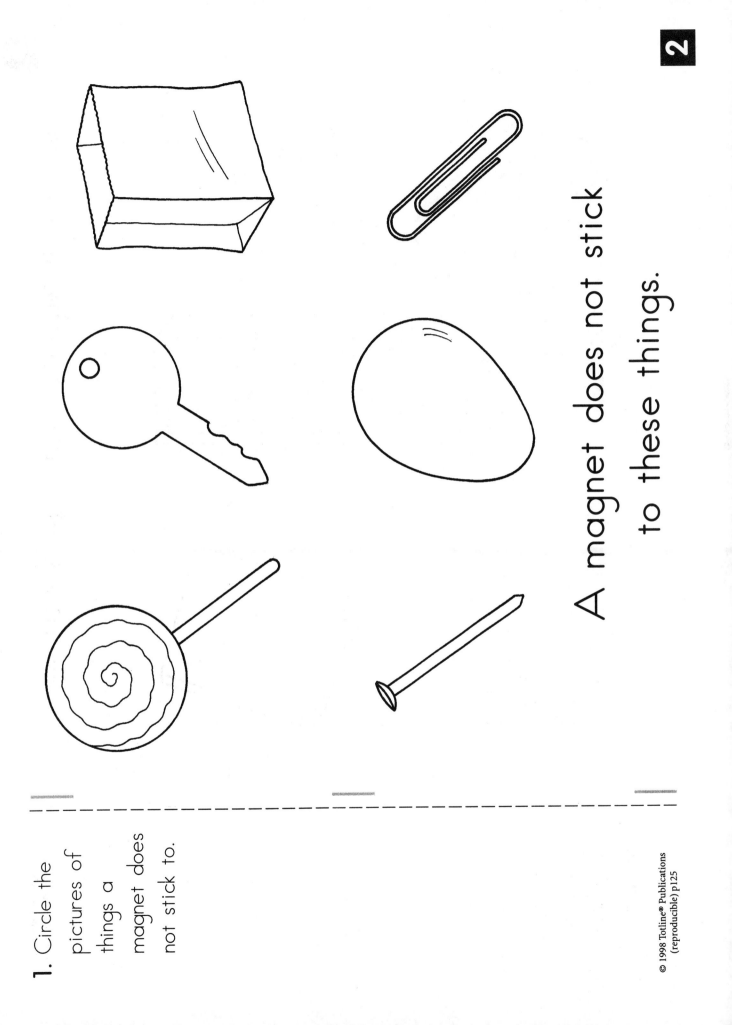

1. Circle the pictures of things a magnet does not stick to.

A magnet does not stick to these things.

1. How many marbles did your magnet catch? Write the number.

2. Color the picture.

I caught _____ magnetic marbles.

3

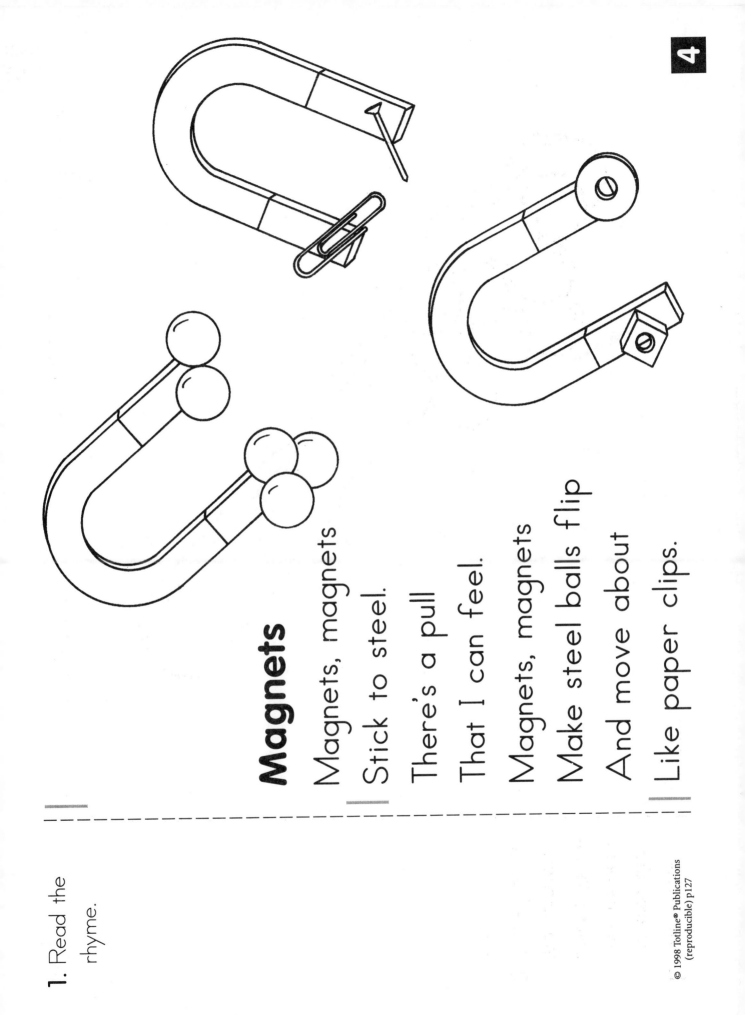

1. Read the rhyme.

Magnets

Magnets, magnets
Stick to steel.

There's a pull
That I can feel.

Magnets, magnets
Make steel balls flip

And move about
Like paper clips.

My Rock Book

By _____

1. Draw the
rocks you
found.

These are the rocks I found.

1

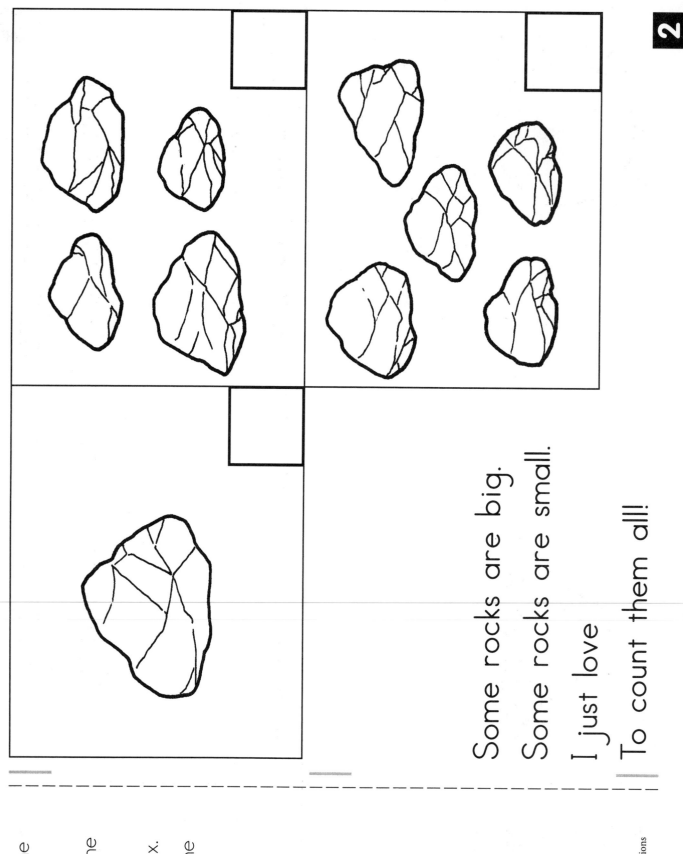

Some rocks are big.
Some rocks are small.
I just love
To count them all!

1. Read the rhyme.
2. Count the rocks in each box.
3. Write the number.

1. Draw some rocks above the ground.
2. Draw some rocks under the ground.

Some rocks are above the ground.
Some rocks are under the ground.

1. Read the
   rhyme.
2. Draw your
   favorite
   rock.

Some rocks are gray.
Some rocks are brown.
Here is the prettiest rock
I found.

My Nature Pattern Book

By _____

1. Color the pictures.

There are many patterns in nature.

1. Finish the
patterns.

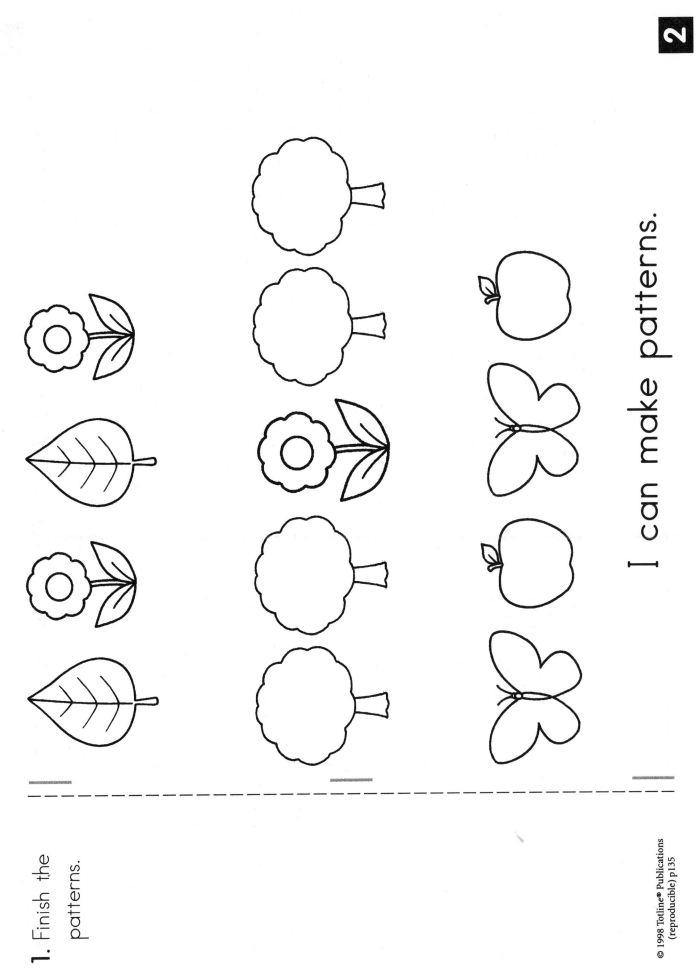

I can make patterns.

© 1998 Totline® Publications
(reproducible) p135

2

1. Trace the lines to finish the pattern.
2. Color the flower.

The petals on flowers are in a pattern.

3

1. Trace the
   lines to finish
   the pattern.
2. Color the
   picture.

Fern leaves are in a pattern.

© 1998 Totline® Publications
(reproducible) p137

My Weather Book

By _____

_____

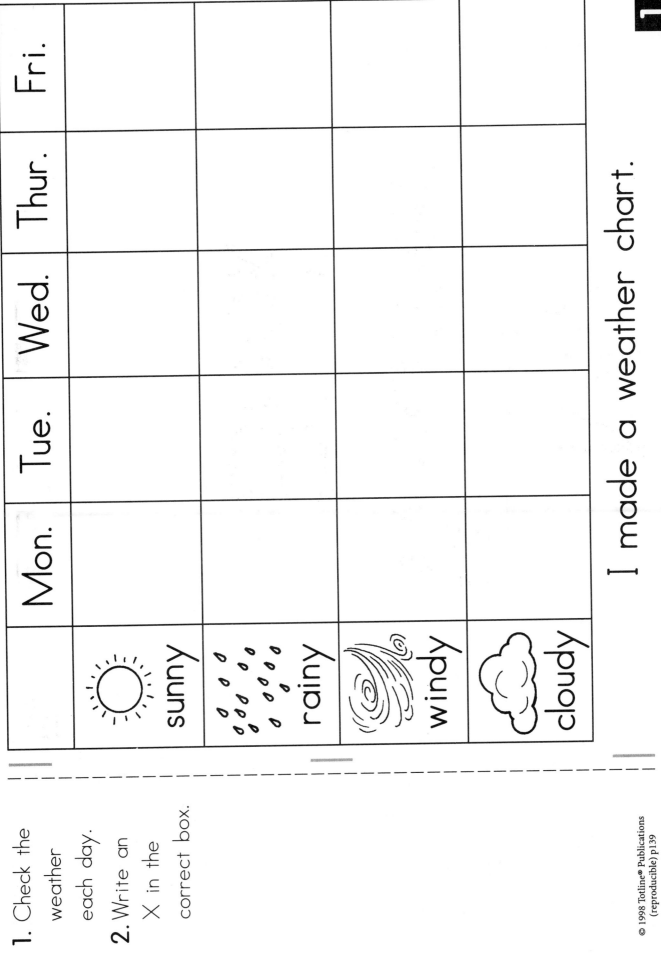

	Mon.	Tue.	Wed.	Thur.	Fri.
☀ sunny					
rainy					
windy					
cloudy					

I made a weather chart.

1. Check the weather each day.
2. Write an X in the correct box.

© 1998 Totline® Publications (reproducible) p139

1

1. How many
sunny days
were there
last week?
Write the
number.

2. Draw a
sunny day.

Last week there were _____ sunny days.

© 1998 Totline® Publications
(reproducible) p140

2

People dress for the weather.

1. Match the clothes to the weather.

1. Read the
   rhyme.
2. Color the
   picture.

Rain on the grass.

Rain on the tree.

Rain on the house.

Rain on me!

4

My
Wind
Book

By _____

1. Circle the
things that
wind can
move.

Wind can move these things.

1

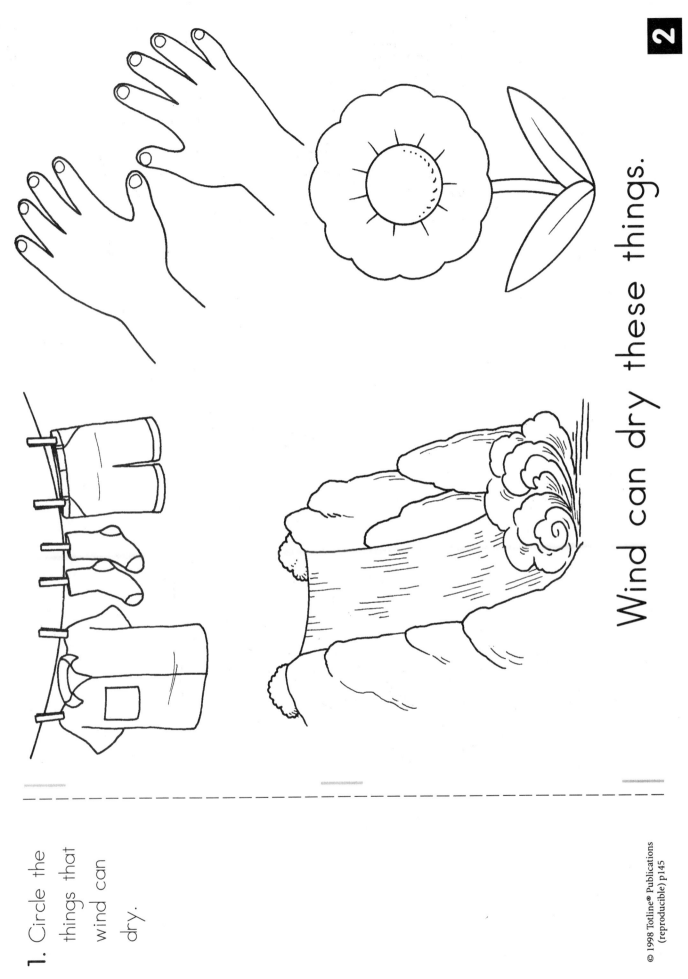

1. Circle the things that wind can dry.

Wind can dry these things.

© 1998 Totline® Publications
(reproducible) p145

1. What do you like to do on a windy day? Finish the sentence.

2. Draw a picture.

On a windy day, I like to _____

3

Wind Is Air

Sung to: "London Bridge"

Wind is air that's moving fast,
Moving fast, moving fast.
Wind is air that's moving fast,
Watch it move the _____.

1. Name one thing wind can move. Write the word.

2. Sing the song.

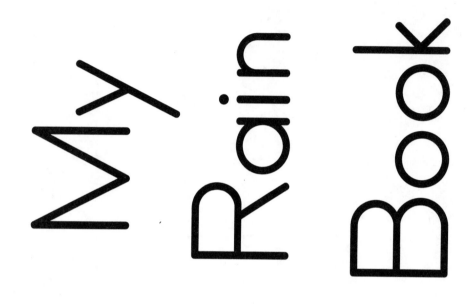

My Rain Book

By _____

1. Why do you like rain? Finish the sentence.

2. Draw a picture.

I like rain because _____.

1

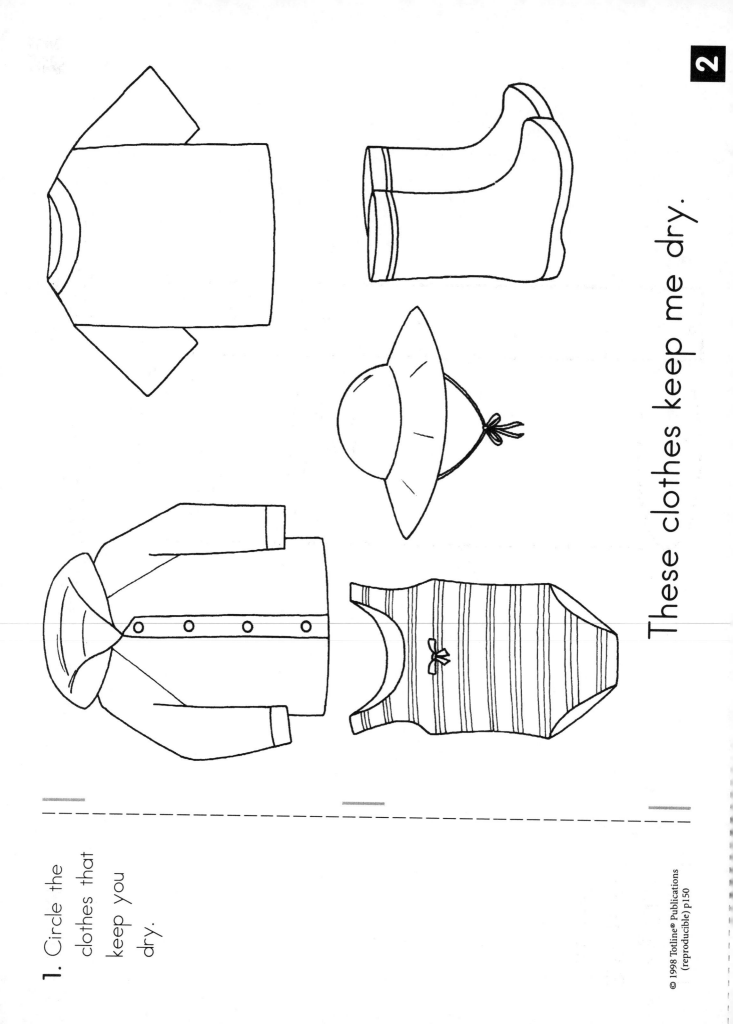

1. Circle the clothes that keep you dry.

These clothes keep me dry.

© 1998 Totline® Publications
(reproducible) p150

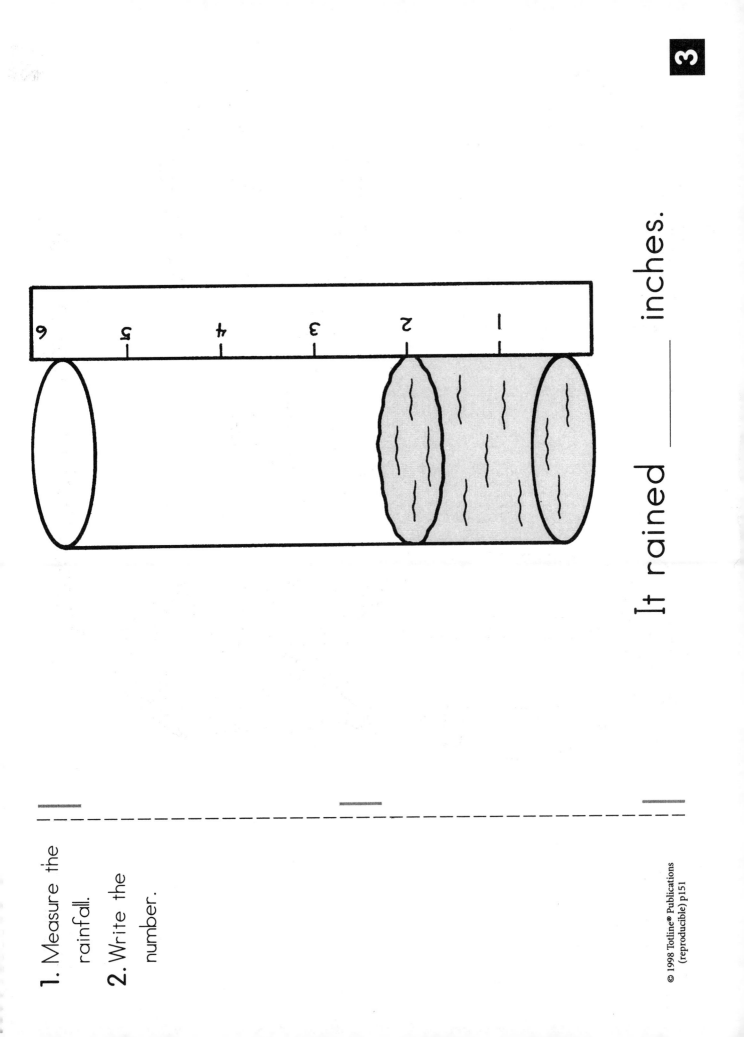

1. Measure the rainfall.

2. Write the number.

It rained _____ inches.

© 1998 Totline® Publications
(reproducible) p151

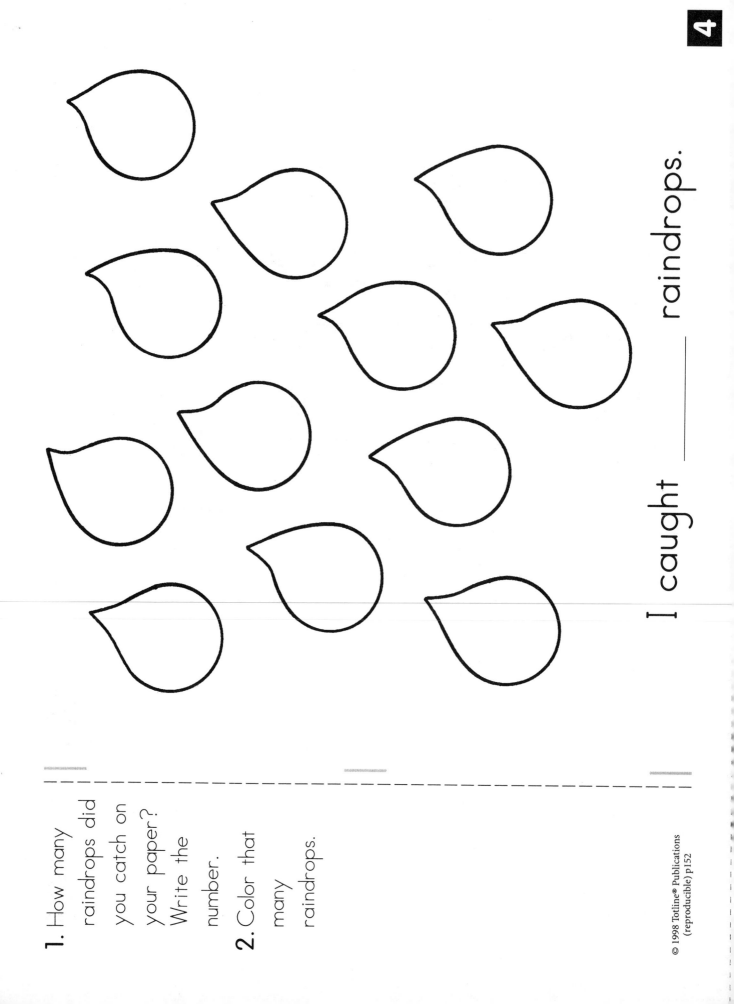

1. How many raindrops did you catch on your paper? Write the number.

2. Color that many raindrops.

I caught _____ raindrops.

4

My Rainbow Book

By _____

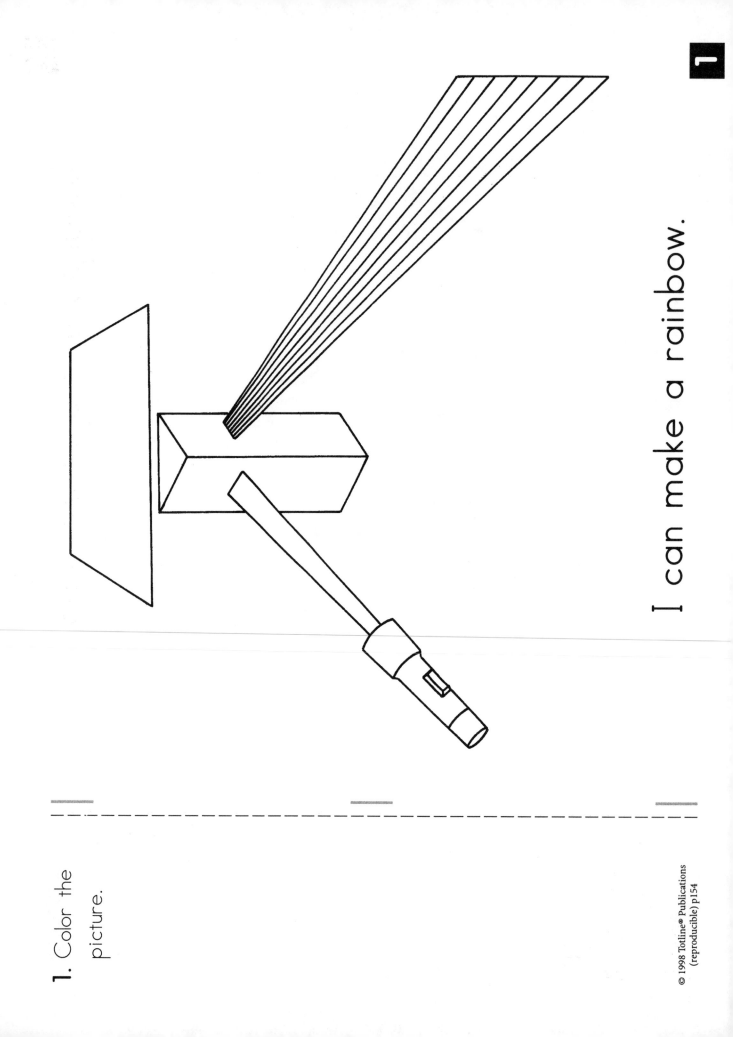

1. Color the
picture.

I can make a rainbow.

1. Draw
   bubbles.
2. Color the
   picture.

I can see colors in bubbles.

1. What is your favorite rainbow color? Write the word.

2. Draw a rainbow.

My favorite color in the rainbow is _____.

1. Read the
   rhyme.
2. Color the
   picture.

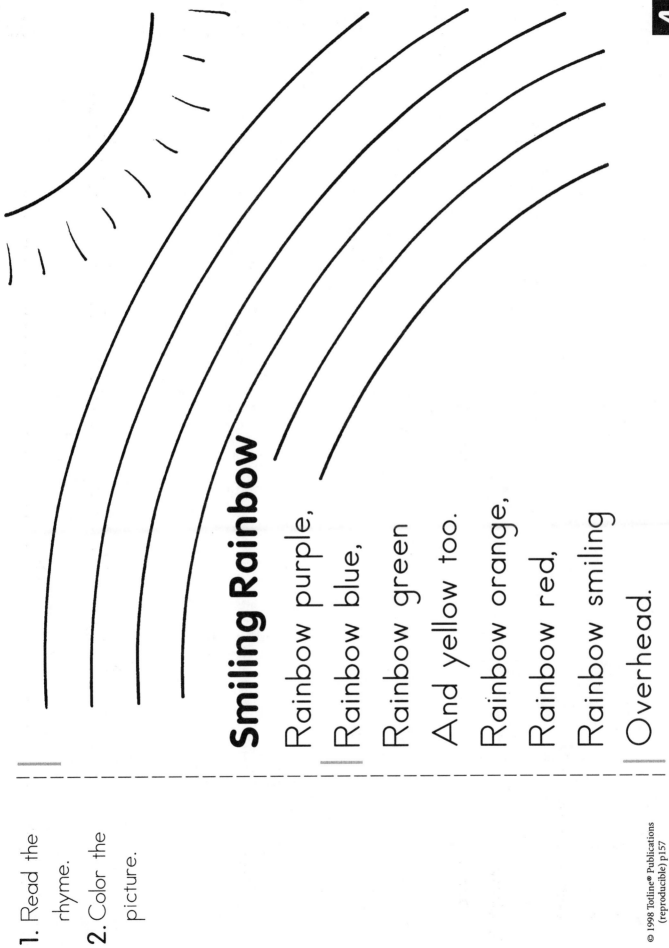

Smiling Rainbow

Rainbow purple,

Rainbow blue,

Rainbow green

And yellow too.

Rainbow orange,

Rainbow red,

Rainbow smiling

Overhead.

© 1998 Totline® Publications
(reproducible) p157

Early Learning Resources

Songs, activities, themes, recipes, and tips

Celebrations

Easy, practical ideas for celebrating holidays and special days around the world. Plus ideas for making ordinary days special.

Celebrating Likes and Differences

Small World Celebrations

Special Day Celebrations

Great Big Holiday Celebrations

Theme-A-Saurus®

Classroom-tested, around-the-curriculum activities organized into imaginative units. Great for implementing child-directed programs.

Multisensory Theme-A-Saurus

Theme-A-Saurus

Theme-A-Saurus II

Toddler Theme-A-Saurus

Alphabet Theme-A-Saurus

Nursery Rhyme Theme-A-Saurus

Storytime Theme-A-Saurus

1•2•3 Series

Open-ended, age-appropriate, cooperative, and no-lose experiences for working with preschool children.

1•2•3 Art

1•2•3 Games

1•2•3 Colors

1•2•3 Puppets

1•2•3 Reading & Writing

1•2•3 Rhymes, Stories & Songs

1•2•3 Math

1•2•3 Science

1•2•3 Shapes

Snacks Series

Easy, educational recipes for healthy eating and expanded learning.

Super Snacks

Healthy Snacks

Teaching Snacks

Multicultural Snacks

Piggyback® Songs

New songs sung to the tunes of childhood favorites. No music to read! Easy for adults and children to learn. Chorded for guitar or autoharp.

Piggyback Songs

More Piggyback Songs

Piggyback Songs for Infants & Toddlers

Piggyback Songs in Praise of God

Piggyback Songs in Praise of Jesus

Holiday Piggyback Songs

Animal Piggyback Songs

Piggyback Songs for School

Piggyback Songs to Sign

Spanish Piggyback Songs

More Piggyback Songs for School

Busy Bees

These seasonal books help two- and three-year-olds discover the world around them through their senses. Each book includes fun activity and learning ideas, songs, snack ideas, and more!

Busy Bees—SPRING

Busy Bees—SUMMER

Busy Bees—FALL

Busy Bees—WINTER

101 Tips for Directors

Great ideas for managing a preschool or daycare. These hassle-free, handy hints are a great help.

Staff and Parent Self-Esteem

Parent Communication

Health and Safety

Marketing Your Center

Resources for You and Your Center

Child Development Training

101 Tips for Toddler Teachers

Designed for adults who work with toddlers.

Classroom Management

Discovery Play

Dramatic Play

Large Motor Play

Small Motor Play

Word Play

101 Tips for Preschool Teachers

Valuable, fresh ideas for adults who work with young children.

Creating Theme Environments

Encouraging Creativity

Developing Motor Skills

Developing Language Skills

Teaching Basic Concepts

Spicing Up Learning Centers

Problem Solving Safari

Designed to help children problem-solve and think for themselves. Each book includes scenarios from children's real play and possible solutions.

Problem Solving Safari—Art

Problem Solving Safari—Blocks

Problem Solving Safari—Dramatic Play

Problem Solving Safari—Manipulatives

Problem Solving Safari—Outdoors

Problem Solving Safari—Science

The Best of Totline® Series

Collections of some of the finest, most useful material published in *Totline Magazine* over the years.

The Best of Totline

The Best of Totline Parent Flyers

A Year of Fun

Age-specific books detailing how young children grow and change and what parents can do to lay a foundation for later learning.

Just for Babies
Just for Ones
Just for Twos
Just for Threes
Just for Fours
Just for Fives

Getting Ready for School

Fun, easy-to-follow ideas for developing essential skills that preschoolers need before they can successfully achieve higher levels of learning.

Ready to Learn Colors, Shapes, and Numbers
Ready to Write and Develop Motor Skills
Ready to Read
Ready to Communicate
Ready to Listen and Explore the Senses

Learning Everywhere

Everyday opportunities for teaching children about language, art, science, math, problem solving, self-esteem, and more!

Teaching House
Teaching Town
Teaching Trips

Beginning Fun With Art

Introduce young children to the fun of art while developing coordination skills and building self-confidence.

Craft Sticks • Crayons • Felt
Glue • Paint • Paper Shapes
Modeling Dough • Yarn
Tissue Paper • Scissors
Rubber Stamps • Stickers

Beginning Fun With Science

Make science fun with these quick, safe, easy-to-do activities that lead to discovery and spark the imagination.

Bugs & Butterflies
Plants & Flowers
Magnets
Rainbows & Colors
Sand & Shells
Water & Bubbles

Teaching Tales

Each of these children's books includes a delightful story plus related activity ideas that expand on the story's theme.

Kids Celebrate the Alphabet
Kids Celebrate Numbers

Seeds for Success™

For parents who want to plant the seeds for success in their young children

Growing Creative Kids
Growing Happy Kids
Growing Responsible Kids
Growing Thinking Kids

Learn With Piggyback® Songs

BOOKS AND TAPES
Age-appropriate songs that help children learn!

Songs & Games for Babies
Songs & Games for Toddlers
Songs & Games for Threes
Songs & Games for Fours

Learning Puzzles

Designed to challenge as children grow.

Kids Celebrate Numbers
Kids Celebrate the Alphabet
Bear Hugs 4-in-1 Puzzle Set
Busy Bees 4-in-1 Puzzle Set

Two-Sided Circle Puzzles

Double-sided, giant floor puzzles designed in a circle with cutout pieces for extra learning and fun.

Underwater Adventure
African Adventure

We Work & Play Together Posters

A colorful collection of cuddly bear posters showing adult and children bears playing and working together.

We Build Together
We Cook Together
We Play Together
We Read Together
We Sing Together
We Work Together

Bear Hugs® Health Posters

Encourage young children to develop good health habits. Additional learning activities on back!

We Brush Our Teeth
We Can Exercise
We Cover our Coughs and Sneezes
We Eat Good Food
We Get Our Rest
We Wash Our Hands

Reminder Posters

Photographic examples of children following the rules.

I cover my coughs
I listen quietly
I pick up my toys
I put my things away
I say please and thank you
I share
I use words when I am angry
I wash my hands
I wipe my nose

If you like Totline® Books, you'll love Totline® Magazine!

For fresh ideas that challenge and engage young children in active learning, reach for **Totline Magazine**—Proven ideas from innovative teachers!

Each issue includes

- Seasonal learning themes
- Stories, songs, and rhymes
- Open-ended art projects
- Science explorations
- Reproducible parent pages
- Ready-made teaching materials
- Activities just for toddlers
- Reproducible healthy snack recipes
- Special pull-outs

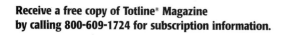